CULTURES OF THE WORLD
MEXICO
by Mary Jo Reilly/Leslie Jermyn

BENCHMARK BOOKS

MARSHALL CAVENDISH
NEW YORK

SULLIVAN COUNTY PUBLIC LIBRARY
SULLIVAN, IN 47882

J
972
Rei
cy

022929

PICTURE CREDITS
Cover photo: R. Kord/H. Armstrong Roberts
Ellen Barone/Houserstock: 43, 58 • Bes Stock: 47 • Steve Bly/Houserstock: 50 • Camera
Press Ltd: 114 • Victor Englebert: 20, 21, 24, 25, 26, 27, 54, 57, 67, 92, 93, 100, 101, 103,
107 • Focus Team Photo Agency: 16, 28 • Getty Images/Hulton Archive: 29, 44, 45, 46
• Rankin Harvey/Houserstock: 42, 80 • Hulton Deutsch: 115 • MC Picture Library: 130
• Photobank Photo Library: 5, 7, 15 • David Simson: 74 • South American Pictures: 6, 9,
10 (bottom), 11, 12, 13, 17, 18, 19 (both), 22, 23, 33, 39, 40, 41, 52, 59, 60, 61, 65, 66,
69, 70, 71, 72, 73, 76, 81, 85, 88, 89, 90, 91, 95, 98, 102, 104, 105, 106, 108, 118, 126
• Liba Taylor Photography: 1, 3, 4, 8, 10 (top), 14, 30, 31, 32, 34, 35, 36, 37, 38, 51, 53,
55, 56, 63, 64, 75, 78, 79, 82, 84, 94, 96, 97, 99, 109, 110, 111, 112, 113, 116 (both), 117,
119, 120, 121, 122, 123, 124, 125 • Stuart Wasserman: 48 • Nik Wheeler: 131

ACKNOWLEDGMENTS
With thanks to Jennifer Vickers of East Carolina University,
for her expert reading of the manuscript.

PRECEDING PAGE
Mexicans march through the streets of Mexico City in a procession to honor the saints.

Marshall Cavendish Corporation
99 White Plains Road
Tarrytown, NY 10591
Website: www.marshallcavendish.com

© 1990, 2002 by Times Media Private Limited
All rights reserved. First edition 1990.
Second edition 2002.

Originated and designed by
Times Books International, an imprint of
Times Media Private Limited, a member of the
Times Publishing Group

Printed in Malaysia

Library of Congress Cataloging-in-Publication Data:
Reilly, Mary-Jo, [date]
    Mexico / by Mary Jo Reilly, Leslie Jermyn.—2nd ed.
        p. cm.—(Cultures of the world)
    Includes bibliographical references and index.
    Summary: Presents the history, geography, economy, people, and social life
and customs of Mexico, the third largest country of Latin America.
    ISBN 0-7614-1363-4
    1. Mexico—Juvenile literature. [1. Mexico.] I. Jermyn, Leslie. II. Title. III. Series

F1208.5 .R45 2002
972—dc21   2001047760

6 5 4 3 2 1

CONTENTS

Outside the modern cities of Mexico, life flows at a more relaxed pace.

The folk crafts of Mexico reflect its unique Indian heritage.

INTRODUCTION

MEXICO IS A LAND of enigmatic civilizations, amazing natural diversity, and colorful cultural traditions. Mexico is home to one of the most advanced pre-Columbian civilizations—the Maya. The Spanish conquest forever changed Mexico's landscape, and, as the richest Spanish colony in the New World, Mexico developed its own cultural blend of indigenous and European culture.

Mexico boasts a great variety of climates and ecosystems. The country's position between North America and the isthmus of Central America gives Mexico an array of climates and ecosystems—from dry desert landscapes to lush tropical jungles. On another level, Mexico also serves as a cultural bridge, where the English-speaking traditions of North America and the Latin traditions of Central and South America meet.

This book takes a close look at Mexico's vibrant history and rich cultural traditions.

GEOGRAPHY

MEXICO IS THE NORTHERNMOST country in Latin America. It is bordered by the United States to the north and Guatemala and Belize to the southeast. Stretching for 2,000 miles (3,218 km) at its widest point, Mexico's shores are washed by the Pacific Ocean to the west and the Gulf of Mexico and the Caribbean Sea to the east. Four times the size of the state of Texas, Mexico is the third largest Latin American country after Brazil and Argentina.

Mexico's early civilizations occupied territory beyond the country's current borders. To the south, these early cultures reached into Guatemala, Belize, El Salvador, and parts of Honduras; to the north, they extended about 300 miles (482 km) north of the Central Valley of Mexico City. This historical area is referred to as Mesoamerica.

Above: **Acapulco, on Mexico's southern Pacific coast, is a beautiful and extremely popular holiday destination for Mexicans and non-Mexicans alike.**

Opposite: **Mt. Popocaté-petl is one of the largest volcanoes in Mexico. The Aztecs once worshiped the volcano as a god.**

GEOGRAPHICAL REGIONS

Most of Mexican land is made up of mountains and plateaus. Two great mountain chains—the Sierra Madre Oriental and Sierra Madre Occidental—run north-south through the country. These two chains form part of a long system of mountains that run up along the west coasts of North America, Central America, and South America. This range splits into two in Mexico. The western arm continues northward and links up with the Rocky Mountains in the United States.

Mexico has an amazingly diverse landscape, consisting of snowcapped mountains and tropical rain forests, beaches and plateaus, barren desert and fertile farmland. The country can be divided into five regions based on climate, land forms, and vegetation patterns.

Desert of Baja California.

THE PACIFIC NORTHWEST This very dry region covers the states of Baja California Norte, Baja California Sur, western Sonora, Sinaloa, and northern Nayarit. Baja California, an 800-mile-long (1,287-km-long) peninsula, is basically a desert.

With so little rain, the landscape of the Pacific northwest is dominated by desert brush and cacti. There are pockets of land where farming occurs, but the land is difficult to cultivate.

The Colorado River delta forms a large lowland in the northeastern part of this region. As the delta grew, it cut off and dried up the northernmost and southernmost parts of the Gulf of California, forming the Imperial Valley in California and the Mexicali Valley in Mexico.

The Pacific northwest's mainland coastal strip is better for farming because it has fertile valleys irrigated by rivers, including the Colorado, Yaqui, and Fuerte. In addition to farmland, these basins support cattle ranches and rich copper and silver mines.

VOLCANOES

Mexico's most famous volcanoes are Popocatépetl and Ixtacihuatl. Popocatépetl, which means "smoking mountain" in the Nahuatl Indian language, has not erupted since 1702, but still releases huge clouds of smoke. Ixtacihuatl, or "sleeping woman," lies next to it. According to legend, the volcanoes are named after two lovers: Popo, a warrior, and Ixta, a princess. When Ixta died, Popo laid her body on one mountain and stood, holding her funeral torch, on the other.

Paricutín, the youngest volcano in Mexico, emerged on February 7, 1943. It grew in the middle of a corn field to 1,700 feet (518 m) in height, poured out tons of lava, and destroyed several villages. It has been dormant since 1952 but can become active again. The most active volcano in recent years is Colima, near the town of Yerbabuena. People in the area have been evacuated repeatedly since 1998, whenever the volcano threatened to blow and destroy nearby towns.

THE CENTRAL PLATEAU This area is located between the two Sierra Madre mountain chains. While the Sonora Desert lies in the arid north, the southern areas contain some of the richest, most fertile farmland in Mexico. Summer rains usually provide good growing conditions for small grains. The western part of the plateau also contains the manufacturing centers of Guadalajara, León, Querétaro, and San Luis Potosí.

Castor oil plants. Cash crops are grown in the southern central plateau, the most fertile region of Mexico.

Above top: **Farming in the Yucatán Peninsula.**

Above bottom: **One of the huge sacred wells of the Mayans.**

THE GULF COASTAL PLAIN AND THE YUCATÁN

The geography of the gulf coastal plain and the Yucatán Peninsula changes gradually from north to south. Both regions are dry in the north, but they get wetter toward the south until they end in tropical rain forests.

The gulf coastal plain is located in the states of Nuevo León, Tamaulipas, Veracruz, and Tabasco. Farming is possible in the northern part of the plain, where the soil is watered by nearby rivers. In contrast, no rivers run through the Yucatán Peninsula. This section is dominated by a limestone plateau with underground channels leading to the sea. Huge pits have formed where the roofs of these channels have fallen in. These pits were once the sacred wells of the Mayan Indians.

THE SIERRA VOLCANICA TRANSVERSAL This region forms a major geological break with the central plateau. Hundreds of volcanic mountains, countless cinder cones, lava flows, ash deposits, hot springs, and other amazing landmarks tell of past and present volcanic activity.

The soil and climate of the Sierra Volcanica Transversal have made the region very attractive to settlers. It has become the most populated area of Mexico, including the capital Mexico City and the cities of Toluca and Puebla. Unfortunately, the basins in this area trap dirty air generated by the cities, making air pollution a major problem.

THE SOUTHERN UPLANDS This region is characterized by steep mountain ridges and deep gorges cut by mountain streams. Several of Mexico's most popular tourist destinations are in this region, including the famed resort city of Acapulco and Monte Albán, the ancient Indian religious center.

The ancient city of Monte Albán lies within the hilly regions of the Southern Uplands. More than 2,000 years old, the city was an important center for the Zatopec people around 300 B.C.

The highest peaks in Mexico are always covered with snow. Frost occurs above 6,000 feet (1,828 m).

CLIMATE

Most people think of Mexico as a hot, dry country, but Mexico also has snowcapped mountains, tropical rain forests, and rich grasslands in addition to deserts.

The Tropic of Cancer cuts Mexico almost exactly in half, putting the southern part of the country in the tropical zone and the northern part in the temperate zone. However, the climate in Mexico is determined as much by altitude as by latitude. Thus the southern tropical zone, which has a wide variety of altitudes, actually includes hot, temperate, and cool areas. And the northern temperate zone has some of the driest deserts to be found anywhere in the world.

Climate

Generally, the coastal lowlands are hot, the plateaus are temperate, and the mountains are cool. Mexicans have named these temperature zones. *Tierra caliente* ("tee-EH-rah cah-lee-EN-tay"), or "hot land," refers to the coastal areas and lowlands. *Tierra templada* ("tee-EH-rah tem-PLAH-dah"), or "temperate land," includes areas from 3,000 to 6,000 feet (914 to 1,828 m). *Tierra fria* ("tee-EH-rah FREE-ah"), or "cold land," is everything above 6,000 feet (1,828 m).

Mexico City, which lies about 7,000 feet (2,133 m) above sea level, is warm during the day and cool at night. The north and northwest of Mexico, which belong to the desert belt of California and Arizona, are very dry.

Rain falls mostly in the mountains near the coasts, leaving the interior of Mexico very dry. The eastern coast gets much more rain than the Pacific coast. Only about 12 percent of the country gets enough rainfall to support the cultivation of crops without irrigation, and almost half the country gets less than 24 inches (61 cm) of rain annually. Except in Baja California, most of the year's rain falls between summer and early autumn.

Mexico's hot and wet season lasts from June to September. December to February are the cool months.

Cactus plants are found in many parts of Mexico where the climate is usually hot and dry.

The wetter regions have
lush tropical forests.

FLORA

Enormous differences in climate naturally result in a wide variety of plant
life in Mexico. The arid northern, northwestern, and central regions
produce plants that are adapted to a limited water supply, such as cactus,
agave, cassava, mesquite, and brush plants.

In the south, east, and on the western coasts, tropical vegetation such
as rain forests, savannah, grazing land, and spiny plants dominate. Some
of Mexico's mountains are snowcapped, some are forested, and others are
completely barren.

Mexico is also home to what is said to be the oldest living thing on the
American continents—a giant ahuehuete tree that Mexicans call *El Arbol
del Tule*, the Tree of Tula.

The poinsettia, the popular floral symbol of Christmas, is native to
Mexico. The plant is usually found in moist, wet, wooded ravines and
rocky hillsides.

FAUNA

Mexico has a rich diversity of animal life that includes species from both North and South America.

Birds, reptiles, insects, and a variety of mammals, including wild sheep, deer, bears, and possums, are plentiful. The tropical rain forests contain such exotic animals as monkeys, jaguars, wild boars, and cougars. The unique volcano rabbit is found only around the Popocatépetl and Ixtacihuatl volcanoes.

Marine life off the coast of Mexico is equally varied, consisting of a wealth of fish and underwater organisms. The northernmost stretch of Mexico's Pacific coast is washed by the Gulf of California, a sheltered sea that opens to the south into the Pacific Ocean. The meeting of the distinct marine environments of the Gulf and the Pacific encourages the growth of a wide variety of fish. Marlin, black sea bass, and sailfish are found far offshore, while smaller species such as porgy and amberjack can be seen closer to the beach.

Perhaps the most spectacular of the mammals off Mexico's coast is the gray whale, which migrates every winter to the waters off Baja California to mate and calve. Virtually extinct 50 years ago, the gray whale has made an amazing comeback. In the waters off Baja California, its favorite breeding ground, the number of whales has risen from 250 in 1937 to 21,000 in recent years.

Another previously endangered mammal that has made a remarkable recovery since the beginning of the 20th century is the elephant seal, which is found near Guadalupe Island.

This young man is holding an iguana, a large lizard found in many tropical countries.

15

HISTORY

THE FIRST SETTLERS IN MEXICO were nomadic hunter-gatherers who crossed the Bering Strait from Asia to Alaska in search of food. Traveling in small groups, they slowly moved south and eventually reached Mexico. Some groups went on as far south as Chile, but those who stayed behind began Mexico's earliest civilizations.

EARLY CIVILIZATIONS

The Olmec Indians developed the first highly civilized culture in Mesoamerica around 1500 B.C. They passed on their culture to other groups through trade and war. Today, the Olmec culture is thought to be the origin of many later Indian empires. The Olmec Indians were a tightly organized, very efficient group ruled by religious and civil leaders. They built religious centers on the gulf coast in southern Veracruz and Tabasco and established colonies in central and southern Mexico.

Above: **The now silent and empty cities of the Mayans are lasting monuments to a great civilization.**

Opposite: **The Mayan ruins of Chichén Itzá on the Yucatán Peninsula.**

The most enduring legacy of the Olmec Indians is their art, especially their stone sculptures. Some of these sculptures are of heads with Asian and African features, suggesting that the Olmec population may have consisted of two ethnic groups. The remains of many of these monuments suggest the Olmec civilization came to a violent end around 400 B.C.

Over the next 1,700 years, many cultures emerged. Some developed and flourished; others faded. Some of the more advanced were the Zapotecs and Mixtecs in southwestern Mexico and Monte Albán; the Tarascans of Michoacán; and the Totonac of Veracruz, who built the famous Pyramid of the Niches in Tajín.

The Mayans were a highly artistic people who built beautiful cities. Many of their monuments have survived more than 1,000 years.

THE MAYANS

Perhaps the most spectacular culture in ancient Mexico, the Mayan civilization was the only one in the Americas to develop an original system of writing used to record chronology, astronomy, history, and religion. Their system of mathematics was an achievement unequaled for centuries in Europe. The 365-day Mayan year was improved upon only in the 20th century. Mayan sculpture and architecture were unmatched in either beauty or dignity.

The Mayan civilization reached its peak about A.D. 200–800. The cities of Palenque and Tikal were the centers of a civilization that numbered over 10 million people. The Mayan culture declined around A.D. 900. Nobody knows why, but it is believed that the Mayans were hit by natural disasters and invaded by hostile groups.

THE AZTECS

The Aztecs emerged faster and became more powerful than any other culture in the history of Mexico. Before their rise, they were a poor nomadic group living in the valleys of Mexico. But by the time of the Spanish conquest in 1521, the Aztec empire covered most of Mesoamerica.

In 1325, the Aztecs arrived on Lake Texcoco near present-day Mexico City. On an island in the middle of the lake, they spotted an eagle perched on a cactus holding a serpent in its mouth. The Aztecs interpreted this as a sign from the gods to settle there. They constructed a city called Tenochtitlán. Today, the eagle with the serpent in its mouth is the symbol of Mexico. It appears on the country's flag and currency.

The first houses in Tenochtitlán were built on rafts in the middle of the shallow lake. One hundred years later, Tenochtitlán became an elegant, complex city, and the Aztecs became a sophisticated society of fierce warriors. Although Aztec society was dominated by the nobles, priests, military, and merchant classes, it made provisions for the common people as well. For example, the education system was more advanced than in any other Mesoamerican civilization.

The Aztecs were an aggressive, violent people dominated by the military and a god of war. The army led many successful wars of conquest, and soldiers were rewarded with land grants and positions of wealth and influence.

Prisoners were either enslaved or sacrificed, because the Aztecs believed this was necessary to please their gods. Methods of sacrifice included drowning, whipping, and tearing hearts out of people while they were still alive.

Above: **Everyday life in the Aztec city of Tenochtitlán (mural by Diego Rivera).**

Below: **These carvings depict the Aztec rain god and Quetzalcóatl, the god of civilization.**

TEOTIHUACÁN

Teotihuacán is the largest, most impressive, and best known of all ancient Mexican religious centers. Built around 300 B.C. by Toltec Indians, it dominated the region until its mysterious decline and fall around A.D. 700. At its peak, Teotihuacán had a population of over 200,000 and was Mexico's largest pre-Hispanic city.

Teotihuacán is laid out in a grid and dominated by the 215-foot (65-m) high Pyramid of the Sun, the third largest pyramid in the world. Other significant buildings in the city include the Pyramid of the Moon and the Temple of Quetzalcóatl.

The people of Teotihuacán were highly skilled artists. Their designs suggest their lives revolved around a complex religious system based on the worship of the sun god, moon goddess, rain god, and god of civilization, Quetzalcóatl, meaning "feathered serpent."

The conquest of the last
Indian empire in Mexico
(mural by Diego Rivera).

SPANISH CONQUEST

In 1519, Hernán Cortés (1485–1547) and about 500 Spanish adventurers called *conquistadores* ("kon-kees-tah-DOH-rehs") set sail for the New World of the Americas in search of treasure. Their arrival stunned the Aztecs, who had never seen ships, horses, or light-skinned people before.

When word reached the Aztec emperor Moctezuma, the highly religious leader thought Cortés must be the god Quetzalcóatl, whom legend said would return to Tenochtitlán that same year. To appease this "god" and to get him to leave, Moctezuma sent Cortés gold, silver, and other riches. When Cortés saw this treasure, he became determined to conquer the Aztecs and have all the wealth for himself.

Had Moctezuma fought Cortés right away, it is unlikely the Spaniards would have survived, as they were vastly outnumbered by millions of Indians. Instead, Cortés found a translator who could communicate with the Indians, kidnapped Moctezuma, and formed alliances with the enemies of the Aztecs. These strategies, together with the Spaniards' sophisticated weaponry, were too much for Moctezuma's people. Though they fought bitterly and bravely, the Aztecs were soon conquered in 1521.

The conquest of the last
Indian empire in Mexico
(mural by Diego Rivera).

Right: **The Monastery of San Agustín. The Spanish conquest soon brought many Catholic missionaries to Mexico.**

Opposite: **The Revolution of 1820. This mural by Diego Rivera depicts the people and the church uniting in the struggle against Spain.**

THE COLONIAL PERIOD

For 300 years under colonial rule, Mexico was governed by the Spanish government, which issued decrees regulating every aspect of life. Spanish nobles ruled the vast lands gained from the decimated Aztecs with a system known as *encomienda* ("en-koh-mee-YEN-dah"), forcing the Indians to give tribute and labor to their Spanish landlords. The Spanish also established a social structure in Mexico. At the top of society were the *peninsulares* ("pay-nin-soo-LAH-rehs"), Spaniards born in Spain, who held political power. Next came the Creoles, who were Spaniards born in Mexico. Below them were the *mestizos* ("mehs-TEE-sohs"), who were of mixed Spanish and Indian blood. At the bottom of the social hierarchy were the Indians.

Another important event was the arrival of Catholic missionaries. Dedicated Catholic friars traveled through Mexico in their quest to convert the masses. Despite the Church's initial idealism, economic opportunities created practices that abused, neglected, and enslaved the Indians.

The combination of imported diseases from Spain and abuses by the Spanish caused a huge number of Indian deaths. In one of the most catastrophic population declines in history, the Indian population fell from about 20 million in 1521 to just two million by 1580.

INDEPENDENCE

Although millions of Indians and *mestizos* suffered abuse because of inequalities in an extremely class-based society, it was the Creoles who started the movement for independence from Spain.

Resentful of Spain's interference in Mexico's burgeoning economy and inspired by ideas of individual rights and freedom from the American and French revolutions, the Creoles began pushing for change. On September 16, 1810, Father Miguel Hidalgo y Costilla, a 57-year-old parish priest from the town of Dolores, began the rebellion with the now famous *Grito de Dolores*, or "Cry of Dolores," demanding independence from Spain. The conflict lasted five years but failed. In 1820, the fight for independence revived, with the Creoles and *peninsulares* banding together. Their new army met with little resistance, and on September 27, 1821, the Treaty of Cordoba was signed, which recognized Mexican independence. A constitution was written and adopted in 1824.

But Mexico was not prepared for independence, having been weakened by 300 years of Spanish domination. During the next 40 years, Mexico had 56 different governments, including periodic rule by dictator Antonio López de Santa Anna (1795–1876) for 30 years. Santa Anna lost half of the country's territory to the United States and was overthrown in 1855 by an Indian named Benito Juárez (1806–1872).

Through its victory in the Mexican War (1846–1848) and subsequent treaty, the United States gained the states of Texas, Utah, Nevada, New Mexico, California, and Arizona, acquiring a territory as large as modern Mexico.

BENITO JUÁREZ AND THE REFORM PERIOD

Benito Juárez, often called the "Abraham Lincoln of Mexico," was a pure Zapotec Indian. He was orphaned as a young boy and raised by a Franciscan friar.

Despite his strict Catholic upbringing, Juárez played an instrumental role in implementing reforms in the Catholic Church. As president of the country (1857–1865, 1867–1872), Juárez oversaw the transfer of political power from the Creoles to the *mestizos*.

The Catholic Church in the 19th century was far more wealthy and powerful than the Mexican government, yet it did little to bring about desperately needed political and social changes. The Church was a conservative force that worked against any reforms that would weaken its power. Conflicts between Church and State eventually led to a three-year civil war called the War of the Reform (1858–1861). Juárez led the liberals to victory and promptly instituted the reforms.

But in 1864 the Church, helped by France, regained power and exiled Juárez. France established its own emperor, a well-intentioned Austrian prince named Maximilian. He tried to institute reforms to help the people, but because he was a foreigner, the people did not trust him.

Three years later, with the help of the United States, Juárez was restored to power, and the reform laws became a permanent part of the Mexican government. When Juárez died in 1872, Mexico had a constitutional and democratic government.

A statue in tribute to President Benito Juárez.

THE PORFIRIATO

The death of Benito Juárez in 1872 led to another period of instability and ultimately to the dictatorship of Porfirio Díaz (1830–1915). Díaz was a *mestizo* who supported Juárez and his reform movement. But when he ran against Juárez for president in 1871 and lost, he claimed the election was fixed and that Juárez shouldn't be allowed to run for president so many times.

Cynically, once Díaz overthrew Juárez's successor in 1876 and took over as head of the government, he ignored his own earlier protests and remained in power for 34 years. His ruthless dictatorship was so significant to Mexican history that this period is called "the Porfiriato."

During the Porfiriato, the economy developed enormously, but social problems worsened. Many people who supported Díaz became rich, but the majority of the Mexican population lived in poverty. By 1910, 100 years after the country's independence, Mexico was a country with great social differences among the people. Most of the land and wealth were concentrated in the hands of about 20 percent of the population. The average peasant owned even less than he or she did before independence.

Porfirio Díaz was president from 1876 to 1911.

Díaz was a very shrewd man, but he caused his own downfall by telling a journalist that he was considering retirement. A relatively unknown Mexican named Francisco Madero (1873–1913) took Díaz at his word and ran against him for the presidency in 1910. At first Díaz did not take his opponent seriously, but Madero's campaign for political reform was so popular and so threatening to Díaz that finally the dictator had him imprisoned until after the election.

Pancho Villa *(opposite)* **and Emiliano Zapata** *(above)* **fought against landed ranchers and the rich. Once seen as bandits, today they are revered as national heroes.**

REVOLUTION TO MODERN TIMES

Francisco Madero strongly opposed violence, but he saw no other way to overthrow Díaz. So in November 1910, he called for rebellion. Revolutionary bands formed throughout Mexico.

In May 1911, Díaz was forced to resign. Madero was subsequently elected president through free and open elections. He realized economic reforms were necessary, but was assassinated in a coup in 1913 before he could implement any changes.

After Madero's death, revolutionary leaders began to quarrel among themselves and with the new president, Venustiano Carranza. Two of these leaders, Emiliano Zapata and Pancho Villa, believed that reform through politics was practically impossible. They gathered Indian armies and forcibly took back land they believed rightfully belonged to the Indians. But Zapata and Villa were killed, and Carranza consolidated his power. Today, Villa and Zapata are national heroes.

In 1917, Carranza called a convention to prepare a new constitution. This constitution, still in effect today, laid the groundwork for a new Mexican nation. It limited presidents to only one term, returned communal land to the peasants, gave the government control over education, the Catholic Church, and farm and oil properties, protected factory workers, and generally guaranteed basic democratic freedoms.

Decades of efforts at reform prevailed, and in 1934, the peaceful election of Lázaro Cárdenas (1895–1970) symbolized the success of the revolution. Cárdenas distributed land, made loans available to peasants, organized workers' and peasants' confederations, and expropriated and nationalized foreign-owned industries, in particular the petroleum industry. His presidency saw the fulfillment of many of the revolution's ideals and provided the stable basis for contemporary Mexico.

GOVERNMENT

MEXICO IS A FEDERAL REPUBLIC divided into 31 states and a federal district containing the capital, Mexico City. The government is based on the Constitution of 1917, which attempts to fulfill the goals fought for during the Mexican Revolution and the following period and to create a structure that both eliminates past abuses and prevents future ones. However, peasant uprisings leading to the deaths of over 100 people in the southern state of Chiapas in December 1993 and January 1994 suggest that Mexico is still a country of great economic inequality and that much needs to be done to improve the lives of the country's poorest citizens.

THE 1917 CONSTITUTION

The constitution divides the government into three branches: executive, legislative, and judicial. It also establishes state governments with elected governors and legislatures.

Under the constitution, the federal government has great power in economic, educational, and state matters. The government used this power to the benefit of the people when it divided privately owned farmlands among the poor and when it set up a national school system. Other uses of this power have been more controversial, such as when the government took over the railroad and oil industries. The federal government also has the authority to suspend a state's constitutional powers and has done so in the past to settle state power struggles. Although the Mexican government still struggles with a weak economy and political corruption, it has become more stable since the establishment of the Constitution of 1917.

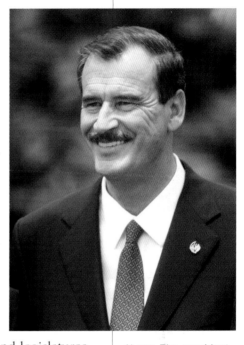

Above: **The president of Mexico, Vicente Fox Quesada.**

Opposite: **Mexico's presidential palace faces the east side of the *zócalo*, one of the world's largest open squares.**

NATIONAL GOVERNMENT

The executive branch of the Mexican government is headed by a president who is elected for a six-year term. There is no vice-president. If a president does not finish his term, the congress chooses a temporary president to serve until a special or regular election is held. The president may not run for reelection.

The legislative branch is called the congress. It is divided into two branches: the senate and the chamber of deputies. The senate has 128 senators, each elected to serve a six-year term. The chamber of deputies has 500 members, each elected for a three-year term. Members of congress cannot serve two consecutive terms.

The judicial system is headed by the Supreme Court of Justice, made up of 21 regular members and five presidential appointees. There are also 32 state-level courts serving the 31 states and the federal district.

STATE AND LOCAL GOVERNMENT

Mexico's states are each headed by a governor. State governors are elected to six-year terms and may not run for reelection. The chamber of deputies in each state has from nine to 25 members. They too are not allowed to serve more than one term in office. The president appoints the chief of Mexico City, the federal district, where the presidential residence, congress, and Supreme Court are located.

Each state is divided into cities or townships called *municipios* ("moo-nee-SEE-pee-ohs"). There are about 2,400 *municipios* in Mexico, each headed by a municipal president and town council. All officers of the local government are elected by the citizens.

THE ARMY

Unlike the armed forces in most other Latin American countries, the Mexican army plays a very insignificant role in governing the republic. Realizing the importance of having the army under their control, Mexican presidents have richly rewarded army loyalty and severely punished acts of betrayal.

As Mexico is unlikely to enter into war with any of its neighbors, Mexican presidents have consistently reduced the army's share of the federal budget. Mexico has one of the lowest ratios of soldiers to population in Latin America. Since 1920, Mexico is the only Latin American country whose government has not experienced an attempted coup.

One of the contributing factors to Mexico's political stability is the army's nonpolitical role.

THE PRI

The strongest political party in Mexico is the Partido Revolucionario Institucional (Institutional Revolutionary Party), referred to as the PRI. It was created in 1929 to serve as the official party for the economic and social goals of the Mexican Revolution. It represents almost every major power group in the nation, including labor unions, the business community, financial interests, and peasant movements.

For a long time, other political parties in Mexico have wielded almost no influence in the national government. Recently, however, this has been changing.

Since its founding, the PRI had won every presidential election by a huge majority. The last election, held in 2000, was an exception. Vicente Fox Quesada won with the Alliance for Change, an alliance of opposition parties to the PRI, including the leading opposition party, the Partido de Acción Nacional (National Action Party), or PAN.

Accusations of corruption have led to violent protests against the PRI. In recent years, the PRI has experienced several electoral defeats to PAN. Mexico is no longer a one-party state; an era of multi-party politics has begun.

U.S.–MEXICAN RELATIONS

Most U.S. citizens don't realize how much the fate of their country is bound with that of Mexico. Due to geographical proximity, what happens in Mexico greatly affects the United States.

The two countries share a 2,000-mile-long (3,218-km-long) unguarded border. While there appears to be no great threat as yet, should unrest in Mexico force the United States to establish border defenses, the cost would be enormous.

Mexico's ability to import from the United States has created 200,000 jobs in the United States. Mexico is the fifth largest market in the world for U.S. goods, and the countries continue to be close trading partners.

Mexican-Americans are an important political force in the United States. Increasingly, U.S. citizens are exposed to Mexican culture and sensitivities, particularly in cities with large Mexican-American populations.

Protest against U.S. interference in Panama. Events occurring in Latin America are of great concern to Mexicans.

ECONOMY

THE MODERN MEXICAN ECONOMY is based on agriculture, industry, and international trade. While agriculture is still important, trade and manufacturing make up the major economic sectors.

DEBT CRISIS

In the 1970s, vast oil reserves were discovered along Mexico's eastern coast. Income from oil production fueled the development of different industries. While the price of oil was high, Mexico borrowed money for construction projects and to finance economic and social development programs. It planned to pay back the debt through oil sales.

However, oil prices fell in the early 1980s, and Mexico found itself in debt without enough money to pay back the loans. The national debt is currently over $150 billion. Mexico has just begun to recover from the worst financial crisis in its history.

NAFTA

Certain sectors of Mexico's economy grew with the implementation of the North American Free Trade Agreement (NAFTA) in 1994. NAFTA established a trading area that included Canada, the United States, and Mexico, with significantly reduced trade tariffs and greater economic cooperation.

Although the United States is already Mexico's most important trade partner, accounting for well over half of Mexico's exports and imports, NAFTA has encouraged an even stronger trade relationship between the two countries. Unfortunately, the benefits of this trade have not been evenly distributed around the country, and some poor Mexicans have tried to resist open trade policies.

Above: **Small cattle ranches are still common in the rural Mexico. Most of these animals will be sold as beef in the markets.**

Opposite: **With available cheap skilled labor, Mexico is industrializing at a rapid pace.**

Forests cover about a fifth of Mexico. The valuable woods found in these forests include ebony, mahogany, rosewood, and walnut.

SOURCES OF REVENUE

Mexicans often talk about the extreme generosity God showed them when He created the country's natural resources: oil, timber, large deposits of gold, silver, and other valuable metals, rivers providing natural irrigation and hydroelectric power, beautiful coastlines, waters filled with fish, and mountains full of game. These natural resources are the foundation of Mexico's economy, with great income-generating potential in mining, agriculture, manufacturing, and tourism.

MANUFACTURING Mexico's transformation from an agricultural economy to an industrial one is largely due to its relatively new oil industry.

Almost half the country's manufacturing activity takes place in Mexico City and its suburbs. This area is Mexico's leading industrial center. Guadalajara and Monterrey are also important industrial cities. The

Monterrey Institute of Technology trains some of the country's best engineers.

Mexico's most important products include farm machinery, chemicals, clothing, iron and steel, processed foods, petroleum, beer, rubber, wood pulp, and paper. The automobile industry makes cars of good quality for export. The National Railroad Car factory supplies most of the cars and equipment used by Mexico's railway system.

The fast growth of manufacturing in Mexico since the 1940s has affected the entire economy. The production of raw materials for new factories has increased; and banking, marketing, and other service industries have expanded. Heavy government spending on construction has provided additional housing for the growing industrial centers. New highways and railroads have been constructed to carry the goods.

Inside a steel factory. Mexico's economy can be described as industrial rather than agricultural.

AGRICULTURE Ever since the early Indians cultivated wild corn, Mexico
has been a predominantly agricultural country. For most of Mexico's
history, the majority of its people lived off the land. Before the revolution
of 1910, most of the land in Mexico was divided into huge estates called
haciendas ("ah-see-EN-dahs") that were owned by wealthy landlords.
After the revolution, the new government divided most of them into *ejidos*
("eh-HEE-dohs"), or communal farms, and distributed them to landless
peasants.

Although only about one-third of Mexican land can be farmed, many
Mexicans manage to survive by growing crops anywhere they can. It is not
unusual, for instance, to see corn growing on a rocky slope.

The kind of crops grown in Mexico varies, depending on the altitude,

rainfall, and temperature of the different regions. The southern part of Mexico's central plateau contains the best farmland. The dry northern part of the plateau is used mainly for cattle grazing, although irrigation projects have developed some cropland.

The wet, hot regions of southern and eastern Mexico and the eastern coastal plains require much work to turn them into productive farmlands. This work includes clearing and draining the land and controlling floods, insects, and plant diseases.

Mexico is self-sufficient in cotton, which is cultivated mainly in the northwestern part of the country. Sisal fiber, obtained from henequen leaves and used for making rope and rugs, is a major product of the Yucatán area.

Harvesting corn. Corn is grown in many parts of Mexico and is the staple food for Mexicans.

This was the richest colonial silver mine in Mexico. Today, with new technology available, it is being exploited again.

MINING It was Mexico's vast amounts of gold and silver that originally attracted Cortés and the Spanish *conquistadores* to its shores. Today, the country still has large deposits of gold and silver as well as copper, lead, zinc, petroleum, iron ore, and sulfur.

The central plateau is the country's most heavily mineralized region. Each year, Mexico mines about one-sixth of the world's total production of silver, making it the world's leading producer of silver.

Mexico has some of the largest oil reserves in the Western Hemisphere, approximately the size of oil reserves in Saudi Arabia. As a result, Mexico has become one of the world's leading producers of petroleum, pumping about a billion barrels each year. The petroleum industry is operated by the government.

A popular beach resort in Mexico.

TOURISM The tourist industry is extremely vital to Mexico's economy. It is often called "the industry without chimneys." Indeed, the Mexican government promotes tourism as an economic asset. Close to 20 million tourists visit Mexico each year. Winter, when the weather is cooler, is the busy season. Typical tourist destinations are Mexico City and the ruins of ancient Mayan and Aztec cities. The most popular beach resorts include Acapulco, Ensenada, Manzanillo, Mazatlán, Puerto Vallarta, Cancún, and Cozumel Island. In the last decade, about 85 percent of visitors to Mexico were from the United States. In addition, about 60 million brief crossings are made each year by Americans for shopping, dining, or auto-repair purposes, rather than for actual vacations.

ENVIRONMENT

MEXICO IS HOME to a wide variety of plants and animals. As a developing country trying to improve its economy and provide for its citizens, however, Mexico faces many challenges when it comes to protecting its natural treasures for future generations.

MEXICO'S TREASURES

Forming a bridge between the continent of North America and the isthmus of Central America, Mexico has unique geographical characteristics. Spanning both temperate and tropical zones, the country is located on a latitude where most of the world's deserts have developed. Different climates and ecosystems occurring at varying altitudes in the mountainous regions have created an incredible degree of biodiversity.

The dry semi-deserts in the north are home to the coyote, puma, armadillo, and deer, while the southern tropical forests support jaguars, ocelots, tapirs, and anteaters. Numerous types of vegetation are found, including deciduous and coniferous forests. Mexico has 35 different species of pine, as well as coastal mangrove forests and semi-arid plains.

Mexico's coastal waters harbor whales, seals, dolphins, and sea lions, and the beaches are breeding grounds for sea turtles. Most species of sea turtle are endangered due to overhunting and habitat loss. Bird life is equally diverse—eagles and ospreys live in the north, while parrots, macaws, and toucans are common in the south. Reptiles abound in the tropical forests, the most spectacular being the Boa Constrictor. Blessed with remarkable diversity, Mexico is a cornucopia of life.

Above: **The beautiful bird of paradise, a plant.**

Opposite: **Mexico boasts rich and diverse ecosystems.**

HUMAN IMPACT

The impact of human activity on the environment has been severe. About two-thirds of the country was forested at the time of the Spanish conquest; only one-fifth remains forested today, and this area is shrinking.

Some of the pressure on forest ecosystems comes from the logging industry; another major contributor is human settlement. As people move into new areas, they clear the land for agriculture. This results in the loss of plant and animal habitats and, eventually, the extinction of species. In the dry north, overgrazing by cattle and excessive irrigation to extend farmlands has led to soil degradation and erosion.

The coasts are also in danger. Spills from oil tankers in the Gulf of Mexico have destroyed marine habitats. Tourism, a growing industry, has brought thousands of people to the beaches, leaving huge amounts of waste to pollute the sand and water. Without proper facilities, waste often gets dumped in the ocean.

Runoff from an oil refinery in Tabasco has polluted nearby streams.

THE MAQUILADORA BORDERLANDS

A Mexican works in the assembly line of an automobile *maquila*.

Pollution is one of Mexico's most critical environmental problems. Places like Tijuana are dangerously polluted with heavy metals, solvents, and acids from *maquila* ("mah-KEE-lah") industries located on the border between Mexico and the United States. *Maquilas* are factories owned by foreigners. The Mexican goverment allows *maquilas* to import parts for Mexican workers to assemble, and then to export assembled products. The first *maquila* industry began in 1965 as part of a program to create jobs in Mexico. The big *maquila* owners are U.S. companies, who find the Maquiladora borderlands a convenient location for transportation of goods to U.S. markets.

Until 2001, *maquilas* were required to export any waste they produced. However, under NAFTA, that rule was dropped. Areas around the Maquiladora borderlands have become industrial dumping grounds, and exposure to industrial pollutants poses a health risk to *maquila* workers.

THE FEDERAL DISTRICT: AN UNHEALTHY PLACE

Mexico City's hazy skyline. This shot was taken around noon on May 15, 1998 after a series of forest fires triggered one of the worst incidents of smog in the city.

Mexico City is nestled in a valley and surrounded on three sides by mountains. This provides perfect conditions for smog to get trapped in the capital. In addition, Mexicans from rural areas swarm to Mexico City—the country's economic hub—looking for work. They crowd the city and suburbs, increasing the amount of waste.

Perhaps the main cause of pollution in Mexico City is emissions from cars, trucks, and buses. The 3 million vehicles in the city contribute some 80 percent of the 5 million tons (5 billion kg) of contaminants released into the city's atmosphere annually. When the No Driving Day program was implemented to ban driving on certain days according to license plate number, wealthy car owners went out and bought themselves another car, thus worsening the city's pollution problem.

Pollution in Mexico City also filters into surrounding areas. Biological waste produced by the city's 16 million residents contaminates river systems flowing out of the valley.

While Mexico City's problems are not unique, they pose a great challenge to the country's environmental agencies and economic planners.

EL VIZCAINO: NURSERY FOR GREY WHALES

The El Vizcaino wildlife sanctuary is found near the center of Baja California, in Baja California Sur State. This area was declared a protected zone in 1971, and in 1993, it became a UNESCO World Heritage Site. Each year, the lagoons located in this area serve as nurseries or kindergartens for female grey whales and their newborn calves. The grey whale lives along the coast of North America, traveling from the Bering Sea off Alaska, where it spends the summers, to Baja California for winter feeding and birthing. This amazing journey of 5,600 miles (9,010 km) is one of the longest known migrations in the animal world.

Grey whales are whalebone whales, meaning that they have long strips of fibrous baleen, an elastic substance, in their mouths to sift out food. Grey whales are unique because, unlike other baleen whales that sift through ocean water, grey whales feed at the bottom of the ocean, straining silt and mud through the baleen as they look for invertebrates to eat. A female grey whale reaches 46 feet (14 m) in length and can weigh 70,000 pounds (31,750 kg), while the male is shorter at 43 feet (13 m). The calves are born at an amazing length of 16 feet (4 m)!

There are about 21,000 grey whales in existence today. But in 1946, they were on the brink of extinction due to whale hunting. El Vizcaino has played an important role in saving the grey whale from certain death.

A Huichol woman weaves a colorful tapestry in Guadalajara Province.

THE REAL TREASURES OF THE SIERRA MADRE

One ray of hope for Mexico's environment is the commitment of the indigenous peoples to protecting their land. This is illustrated in the efforts of the Huichols, for example. The Huichols are indigenous Indians who have succeeded in preserving most of their culture and environment due to their isolation in the traditionally impenetrable Sierra Madre mountains. However, outsiders found their way to the mountains and began destroying the environment. As water was drained away to support the thriving city of Guadalajara, the forests of the Sierra Madre began to disappear, as did animals living in the region, such as the white-tale deer.

The Huichols, seeing themselves as stewards of the planet, decided to take action. In 1986, they made a 600-mile (965-km) pilgrimage to Mexico City to ask the government for a white-tale deer from the National Zoo; they were given 20 to revive the white-tale deer population in the Sierra Madre mountains. Huichol elders now work with the National Indigenous Institute on educational, economic, and health programs. The Cousteau Society has also started the Punta Mita program, which develops environmentally safe tourism in the area. The Huichols were awarded Mexico's National Ecology Prize in 1988 for their genuine efforts to save the environment.

PIRATES OR PROSPECTORS?

An important reason for preserving the natural environment is that it may hold many undiscovered cures for illnesses. This is particularly true of plants in tropical rain forests, which have not yet been fully explored by scientists. Indigenous groups that have lived in these regions for thousands of years know a great deal about tropical wildlife.

The Maya of the state of Chiapas is one such group. Western scientists and pharmaceutical companies have realized that indigenous knowledge of the natural environment may hold the key to curing diseases such as arthritis and AIDS. The issue at stake is the rights to ownership of this information. Some argue that indigenous people own their knowledge, while others say that pharmaceutical companies have the right to gain profit from the drugs they make based on indigenous information; still others argue that this knowledge should be shared freely for the benefit of all humanity.

There is an ongoing conflict between the Maya and industrial groups eager to explore or 'prospect' for new drugs in Chiapas. Mayan folk healers fear that scientists will claim ownership over what really belongs to the Maya. The United Nations' Treaty on Biodiversity states that indigenous interests must be protected, but many nations, such as the United States, have not signed this treaty. There may be no easy answer to the question of ownership of information, but it is clear that it is in everyone's interest to protect and preserve the environment.

"The Huichols teach us that man must be a steward of the Earth, he must feel in his heart the pain of the wounded animal, the crushed blade of grass. For all souls are linked."

—Charmayne McGee, author of So Sings the Blue Deer *(1997)*

SOLUTIONS

Mexicans are aware of the natural treasures they possess and make efforts to protect them. The government has designated a number of protected areas around the country in an effort to preserve the country's flora and fauna. But Mexico cannot solve its pollution problem without outside help. Pressure to produce goods for export forces Mexican industries to produce cheaply in order to meet demand and beat competition. Cheap production methods and outdated technology pollute the environment. As a NAFTA member, Mexico needs the support of the United States and Canada to gain access to safer technologies and reduce the pressure to produce goods cheaply at the cost of the environment.

MEXICANS

THE MEXICAN POPULATION is a unique blend of peoples. There are some 200 different Indian groups and pockets of people of African or European descent.

Mexico is an extremely class-conscious society. The Spanish conquest was followed by centuries of oppression of the indigenous population. After achieving independence, the new ruling class of Creoles and *mestizos* continued to discriminate against Indians. Not until after the Revolution of 1910 were efforts made to advance the position of the Indians socially and economically. But while the government tries to promote Indian accomplishments and culture, Mexican society still treats pure-blooded Indians as social inferiors.

Many Indians have a deep-seated sense of inferiority stemming from various historical and social factors. For example, the Mexican ideal of beauty, as perpetuated in the media, encompasses light skin, blue eyes, and blond hair—typically European features. Also, high rates of poverty and illiteracy among Mexican Indians make them the most vulnerable group during economic recession. In addition, the practice of human sacrifice and cannibalism among some Indian groups before the Spanish conquest can be a source of shame to present-day Indians.

Another contributing factor to the apparent powerlessness of Indians in Mexican society may be their unaggressive attitude and behavior. The Indians try to accept life as it is; the *mestizos* try to dominate and control. The Indians are community-oriented; the *mestizos* are strongly individualistic. The Indians believe they are controlled by fate and destiny; the *mestizos* respect the qualities of a strong individual personality.

Above: **A regal-looking Indian woman. Mexican Indians look distinctively Asian.**

Opposite: **A charming *charro* smiles before the start of a Mexican rodeo.**

INDIANS

Mexican Indians are descendants of a pre-Hispanic people who migrated from Asia to America. Evidence of Mexico's Asian roots exists even today. Many Mexicans still have Asian features, and in some very fundamental ways native Mexican culture and people are more Asian than Western.

Mexico has eight to 10 million Indians, divided into 56 recognized ethnic and language groups, with over 100 different dialects. Most of these groups live in the central plateau, in the southern Pacific coastal states of Oaxaca, Chiapas, and Guerrero, and in Yucatán and Veracruz on the gulf coast.

The largest Indian group are the Nahua, who number over 1.5 million.

Olmec head sculptures with African features. Whether people with these features actually lived in Mexico is a mystery. It is believed that the Olmecs had no contact with any foreign civilizations as their languages were un-like those in other parts of the world, and no relics from other civilizations have been found.

The Nahua are descended from the Aztecs. The Mayans, with a population of around 750,000, are the next largest group. There are also about 350,000 Zapotec, 300,000 Mixtec, and 200,000 Totonac. These are descended from the better known pre-Spanish civilizations.

Other groups include the Otomí, Mazahua, Huastec, Tzotzil, Tzeltal, and Huichol. Some groups, like the Lacandones, Kiliwas, Cucapas, and Paispais, have been reduced to a few dozen families. Most have absorbed aspects of *mestizo* culture, but a few still live in almost total isolation.

Some remote Indian villages are cut off from many modern facilities, such as telephones and electricity. The lives of the villagers have remained virtually unchanged since the arrival of the Spanish. Many Indians still sleep on thin straw mats or in hammocks. Their villages form a striking contrast to the sophisticated, cosmopolitan areas of Mexico City and Guadalajara.

In Mexico, indigenous Indians still suffer from discrimination.

Mestizos are people of Spanish and Indian heritage.

MESTIZOS

In contrast to the early colonists of North America, who brought entire families to the New World to start a new life in the hope of escaping religious persecution at home, the Spanish conquerors were adventurers out to claim new lands for themselves and the Spanish crown. There was no place for women or children in their often war-like adventures, so they left their families in Spain. Many of them married Indian women and settled in the colonies. Children born to these Spanish-Indian couples became the first *mestizos*.

Today, 60 percent of the Mexican population is *mestizo*. No other former Spanish colony in Latin America is as thoroughly *mestizo* as Mexico is. Large Indian populations still exist in Central and South America, but the ruling classes are usually made up of pure-blooded Europeans.

Although the colonies of other countries in the region were similarly shaped by migrants from Europe and later by slaves from Africa, only in Mexico did complete religious, political, and ethnic mixing take place.

THE HUICHOLS: A WINDOW TO THE PAST

A group of around 15,000 Huichol Indians live in the Sierra Madre mountains. In the past, this remote location in such rugged mountainous terrain protected the Huichols from the abuse of the *conquistadores* and the influence of the Catholic missionaries.

Having preserved their pre-Columbian traditions to modern times, the Huichols offer a fascinating window to Mexico's pre-Spanish past. Huichol shamans practice healing rituals as they have for generations. Perhaps their survival is partly the result of their focus on tradition.

The Huichols are most popularly known for their ritual use of *peyote*, a type of cactus that has hallucinogenic effects. *Peyote* is used for planting, harvesting, and deer hunting ceremonies. However, the soil and climate of Huichol land are not ideal for growing *peyote*, so the Huichols make an annual pilgrimage to the desert of San Luis Potosí to find the cactus.

So far there has been no serious threat to the Huichol way of life, whether from *mestizos* or tourists. The Mexican government has also been sympathetic to the Huichols' desire to preserve their ancient culture.

POPULATION PROBLEMS

Mexico is home to more than 100 million people. It is the most populous country south of the Rio Grande after Brazil. The Mexican population doubled between 1960 and 1980 largely due to improved health care for the poor. Beginning in 1930, the government introduced effective methods of treating childhood diseases in Mexico's poorer areas. Consequently, more children survived to adulthood.

Rapid population growth without careful government planning and fair distribution of resources means that some people live in dire poverty without access to basic services.

However, people still thought many of their children would die young, so they continued to have large families.

Due in part to the introduction of birth control in 1976, the rate of population growth dropped from 3.5 percent before 1980 to 1.5 percent in 2000. Also, people have begun to realize that more of their children have a chance at life, so they have fewer babies. However, due to the uneven distribution of resources like health care, education, and land, the Mexican standard of living varies greatly among economic classes.

DRESS

In the cities and large towns, Mexicans wear clothing similar to that worn in the United States. Village wear, however, is very simple and practical, designed to meet the needs of a particular region and climate. Often the designs are hundreds of years old.

In central and southern Mexico, village men usually wear plain cotton shirts and pants and leather sandals called *huaraches* ("wah-RAH-chays"). Wide-brimmed felt or straw hats called *sombreros* ("sohm-BRAY-rohs") offer protection against the sun, and *ponchos* ("PON-chohs") protect them from the rain. At night, men wrap themselves in *serapes* ("say-RAH-pays"), or colorful blankets hung over one shoulder during the day.

Village women wear blouses and long, full skirts and usually go barefoot. They use shawls called *rebozos* ("ray-BOH-sohs") to cover their heads. Mothers also use *rebozos* to secure their babies on their backs.

Mexican Indians are famous for their beautiful homemade fabrics. Weaving styles are different throughout Mexico, and it is possible to identify an Indian's regional homeland by the color and design of his *poncho* or *serape*.

Some Indians have traditional clothing that is usually worn on holidays or for other celebrations. Indians in Oaxaca wear large straw capes. Women on the Isthmus of Tehuantepec wear a wide, lacy white headdress called a *huipil grande* ("wee-PEEL GRAHN-day") on holidays. Mayan women in the Yucatán wear long, loose white dresses embroidered around the neck and bottom hem.

Traditional Mexican dress consists of colorfully woven shawls and blankets. This woman carries her baby with the help of a *rebozo*.

Perhaps the best known of all traditional Indian clothing is the *china poblana* ("CHEE-nah poh-BLAH-nah"). Worn by women, usually when performing the Mexican hat dance, it consists of a full red and green skirt decorated with beads and other ornaments, a short-sleeved, colorfully-embroidered blouse, and a brightly-colored sash.

LIFESTYLE

THERE IS A VERY BIG DIFFERENCE between city life and village life in Mexico. Most Mexican cities are cosmopolitan, with inhabitants who lead lifestyles similar to those led by people living in many cities in Europe and the United States. Values are generally more liberal in Mexico's urban areas than in the villages. Women have far more opportunities to pursue higher education, jobs are easier to find, and education and health care are more accessible.

In contrast, life on farms and in villages has changed very little over the last century. Many farmers live in small villages located near their fields. Still following ancient customs and living as their ancestors did before the Spanish arrived, some Indian villagers resent the imposition of *mestizo* culture.

A large number of Mexican cities and towns began as Indian communities. After the Spaniards conquered Mexico, they rebuilt the communities and made them more like Spanish towns. The central church and main public and government buildings were built around a public square called a plaza. The plazas were meant to serve as the center of city life, much as they do in Europe.

In addition to a plaza, almost every village, city, and town in Mexico has a marketplace. Going to the market is an important activity for people in farm areas. Men, women, and children take whatever they wish to sell or trade and either rent stalls at which to display their goods or simply spread their merchandise on the ground. Then they spend the day at the market visiting with friends or selling their wares.

Above: **In the rural areas of Mexico, lifestyles have not changed much since the beginning of the 20th century.**

Opposite: **A Mexican family at the Plaza de Armas in Guadalajara.**

59

The average Mexican family consists of five or six members, the father being the breadwinner and usually the head of the family.

FAMILY: THE CORE OF SOCIETY

Mexican families form the core of the country's social structure. Indeed, the strength of the family forms the foundation of Mexico's continued political stability.

The Mexican family includes both immediate family and extended family—aunts, uncles, grandparents, and cousins. Families are extremely self-sufficient and closed to outsiders, except for very close friends who are considered part of the family. The family provides emotional and economic support to each of its members. Family-run farms, stores, shops, restaurants, and other businesses together employ millions of people. Even the poorest families offer their members more economic security in times of hardship than the government does.

The social life of family members revolves around being with relatives. Children have so many brothers, sisters, and cousins that they may not need to play with other friends.

The Mexican family structure has survived a great deal of change in the last 60 years. Growing rural populations have been forced to migrate to the cities in search of work. Children of middle-class and wealthy families have begun learning foreign languages and adopting foreign customs and are traveling much more than their parents ever have. Industrialization and urbanization have drastically changed provincial lifestyles. The Catholic Church has lost much of its influence as people have become less religious. But through it all, the family unit has survived. Over 90 percent of Mexicans still live in some kind of family group.

Older sisters often help their mother look after younger siblings.

The average Mexican household consists of five or six people. Often, several generations of the same family live together. The head of the family is often the grandfather or great-grandfather. The father is the unquestioned figure of authority. Unfortunately, sometimes his job or his *machismo* ("mah-CHEES-moh") leads him to neglect his wife and family. Also, he feels that the task of maintaining the home is solely the woman's duty. A mother is usually adored by her children, as she is the one who gives them all the care and attention.

STAGES OF LIFE

CHILDHOOD AND ADOLESCENCE Mexican girls do not have nearly as much freedom as girls in the United States. Peasant girls are assigned household chores from the time they are very young, and by the time they are seven or eight, most are helping to care for their younger brothers and sisters. In Mexican villages, little girls can often be seen carrying their baby brothers or sisters on their backs.

Rural peasants think of cities as sinful places and are extremely reluctant to allow their daughters to move to the cities. The only possible exception would be if the girl can move in with a relative who has already settled in the city. Mexican boys are usually doted on by their mothers. Unlike girls, boys are allowed more independence and free time, as they are not expected to do household chores. In the villages, though, sons normally help in the fields.

In both villages and cities, most young men and women live at home until they are married. Many daughters of wealthy families may live and study abroad. Yet upon their return, they go back to their parents' home.

MARRIAGE Marriage in Indian villages is still very traditional. Village girls usually marry between age 14 and 16, and village boys in their late teens. Marriages are still arranged in some Indian communities, and the bride's family is expected to pay a dowry.

In the rural southeast, custom requires that the male members of the family object to a woman's leaving home. Thus, she is often taken forcefully by her boyfriend, with peace eventually being restored between the families only after the couples' first child is born.

Huichol girls marry when they are as young as 13. Men commonly have more than one wife, and adultery is tolerated in men.

A Mexican wedding.

Poor Mexicans usually cannot afford a marriage license but still live together as husband and wife. These marriages are considered valid in the eyes of their peers. Some Indians wear feathers of small birds in their hair to indicate that they are married.

PREGNANCY AND CHILDBIRTH Birth control is not widely practiced in Mexico, and many women become pregnant shortly after getting married. If an unmarried village girl becomes pregnant, the father of her child will usually marry her. This is not necessarily the case, however, in the cities, and the number of unwed mothers is much higher in the urban areas than in the villages.

DEATH AND FUNERALS Mexicans celebrate the Day of the Dead every November with picnics at the cemetery. They eat on the graves of their

A funeral in procession. People believe that the spirit or soul of a person never dies.

ancestors, believing that departed souls return on that day. Many Mexicans believe the living can communicate with the dead. To them, the past is never dead, and death is not the end but a phase in an infinite cycle.

The Mexican view of death goes back to the religion of the Aztecs and the influence of the Catholic missionaries. The Aztecs believed the death of a sacrificial victim had special significance, and they offered human sacrifices to please the gods. While the Catholic missionaries also believed in the special significance of the death of a sacrificial victim, they believed that what happened to the individual after death depended on how he or she lived, and they shifted the emphasis on human sacrifice to an emphasis on prayer and good works.

MACHISMO

Machismo refers to the strong sense of masculine pride felt by many Mexican men. They constantly try to prove their manhood by, for example, having mistresses, being domineering and overly protective of women around them, paying the bill in restaurants even if they cannot afford it, and having many children to demonstrate their fertility. They feel they must be aggressive and project an image of strength.

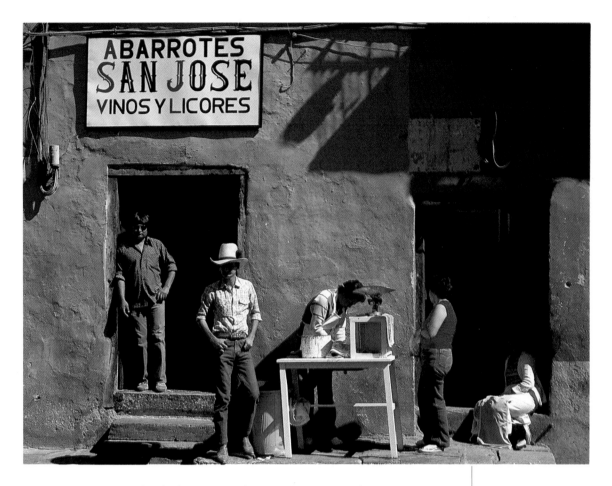

Many Mexicans think, however, that machismo is a front men put up to hide their insecurities. Mexican men often try to cover up their fears with ostentatious displays of manliness, and it is believed they do this mainly to impress other men.

But the most damaging effects of machismo on Mexican society may be manifested in the adulterous habits of married men and in the way they treat women. Machismo has been a contributing factor in the breakdown of many marriages and in the occurrence of many pregnancies, which partly explains the country's high birth rate.

Machismo has not been all bad, however. Being macho has not prevented Mexican men from being gentle with children and affectionate toward friends, and even the most macho of men may cry in public.

It is common for young girls to help with family work, especially in the home or in the family business.

WOMEN

Although women in Mexico are generally treated as subordinate to men, their role in society is crucial. Despite the bravado of Mexican machismo, Mexican women are the pillars of the family. Mothers pass on to their children religious beliefs, myths and legends, and customs and traditions that form the foundation of family and community life.

Mexican attitude toward women is less liberal than in the United States and northern Europe. In Mexico, a woman's principal assets are thought to be beauty, compassion, and tenderness. She is expected to show her husband obedience and provide him with pleasure, assistance, and counsel. She is expected to always treat him with respect, as he is the one who supports and protects her.

As in most Latin American countries, peasant women in Mexico do very little outside the home besides going to the market. At home, they prepare the food, wash the clothes, and raise the children. They usually have many children, not only because birth control is difficult to obtain, but because

A village communal laundry.

they need the extra hands to help with the work. Having many children also assures them of having many providers when they grow old. Traditional husbands also believe it is important to produce many children to show their masculinity.

Peasant women rarely talk to strangers and never join their husbands in entertaining visitors. The only exception may be grandmothers, especially those whose husbands have died. Grandmothers are revered and so may do "unladylike" things in public, such as drinking and smoking.

In urban areas, middle-class and wealthy women have much more freedom than those from poorer families. Economic conditions have made it necessary for more women to go to work. Having jobs enables them to support themselves and walk out of unhappy marriages that they would otherwise have been forced to stay in. There has also been a steady increase in the number of women attending universities, which has enabled them to gain higher-income jobs in the public and private sectors.

CUSTOMS

GREETINGS AND FAREWELLS In Mexico, greetings and goodbyes are quite warm and affectionate and always involve a handshake. Women kiss each other on the cheek when introduced and whenever they meet. These formalities are very important, and it is considered rude to ignore them. The main form of greeting, especially between men, is the *abrazo*, or embrace. It follows a strict pattern. First comes the handshake, followed by the embrace and two strong coordinated pats on the back, and finally, a second handshake and a pat on the shoulder.

COMPADRE* AND *COMADRE Literally, these words translate as "co-father" and "co-mother" and refer to the godfather and godmother of one's children. *Compadres* ("kohm-PAH-drays") and *comadres* ("koh-MAH-drays") often support each other in times of need.

Younger men sometimes call their close friends *compadre*. Although this is often done in a casual manner, in some cases it carries the connotation that they feel so close to a certain friend that they would gladly welcome him into their family as the godfather of a son or daughter.

THE *MAÑANA* SYNDROME Mexicans have their own unique sense of time. It can be very frustrating to people who are unfamiliar with it. They can be either hours late for appointments or not show up at all. They believe anything being enjoyed at the moment is not worth ending for the sake of a serious appointment.

It is also difficult for Mexicans to say no. They may accept invitations and make appointments that they have no intention of keeping, because they believe it is ruder to refuse an invitation than to not show up for it. This attitude is called the *mañana* ("mah-NYAH-nah") syndrome.

Mañana *is a Spanish word meaning "tomorrow." A* mañana *attitude prevails in many Spanish-speaking cultures.*

Mexicans are a warm and helpful people.

POLITENESS Mexicans are very polite. When asked, "Where are you from?", they will often answer *"Donde tiene su casa"* or "Where your home is," implying that "my home is your home."

One must be careful when admiring another's possessions. The owner of the item often will offer it to the admirer as a gift. Envy is a discouraged emotion among Mexicans.

SIESTAS Most Mexicans living in villages and rural areas eat a big meal called *comida* ("koh-MEE-dah") in the afternoon and take a nap, or *siesta* ("see-EHS-tah"), until about 4 P.M. During this time, shops close and things become very quiet. Schoolchildren also go home for a *siesta* and resume classes in the afternoon. In cities, hectic schedules are steadily eliminating the *siesta* custom.

SOCIAL CONDITIONS

Wealthy Mexican citizens lead lifestyles comparable to those of the elite of any country. Mexico also has a fairly large, comfortable middle class. However, the majority of the population, consisting mostly of indigenous Indians, live in poverty, some barely making ends meet. Mexico is formally committed to improving social conditions; the government spends billions of dollars annually on social welfare programs.

HEALTH Although improving social assistance and health services have greatly reduced Mexico's death rate over the last 70 years, the health of the rural and urban poor is still far below the government's minimum standards. Malnutrition is common and is the cause of many diseases, such as rickets and anemia. There are also many cases of tonsilitis, influenza, and respiratory diseases. The Mexican's average life span is about 75 years for women and 68 years for men.

Spanish is the language of instruction in schools.

HOUSING The housing crisis, particularly in the cities, is one of the most serious of Mexico's social problems. In addition to a major housing shortage, there is the problem of poor housing. Two-thirds of the population live without an adequate water supply or a proper drainage system and sometimes without electricity.

WELFARE SERVICES Mexicans do not receive unemployment or welfare benefits. If they do not have a stable job, they have to find other means to make a living or rely on their family to survive.

EDUCATION Since the Revolution of 1910, Mexico has invested large amounts of money in its education system, successfully helping many Mexicans improve their lives. But the growing population creates new problems for the education system, since more schools and teachers are required. The average Mexican attends school for only five years, and 10 percent of Mexican adults are illiterate.

The average Mexican village does not have asphalt roads, proper drains, or running water.

WAGES AND COST OF LIVING The average Mexican man works from dawn to dusk. However, he is paid low wages and often does not earn enough to feed or house his family properly. As a result, many women and children have to do odd jobs to supplement the family income.

A law which was introduced in 1934 requires employers to pay their employees at least the minimum wage. This law, however, is rarely observed. In any case, the minimum wage is not enough to support a family. Workers are entitled to ask for a raise twice a year, but the typical increase in wages rarely covers the increase in cost of living.

CASA MEXICANA

Mexican suburbs are full of modern houses and apartment buildings. The older parts of the cities have rows of Spanish colonial-style homes. Most of these houses are made of stone or adobe brick and have patios located at the center of the house. These patios served as the center of life for the Spanish families that inhabited these houses.

Poorer Mexicans live in slum shacks or rooms with almost no furniture. *Petates* ("pay-TAH-tays"), or straw mats, serve as beds. Clay bowls serve as dishes. Entire families may live in a one-room house. The shapes, styles, and building materials of these homes vary according to the requirements of the climate. Homes on the dry central plateau are made of adobe, cement, or stone, with flat roofs of red tiles, sheet metal, or straw. Some have hard-packed dirt floors, one door, and few or no windows. Cooking is done on a stove placed against an outside wall or over a fire on the floor.

In areas with heavy rainfall, most houses have walls made of poles covered with a mixture of lime and clay. This mixture lasts longer in the rain than adobe does. The houses have sloping roofs. In Yucatán, most Indian houses are rectangular in shape but have rounded corners. Roofs are made of neatly trimmed palm leaves.

MEXICO CITY

Mexico City, the capital of Mexico, is one of the largest cities in the world, with an estimated population of around 20 million. The city was founded soon after the Spanish conquest, on the site of Tenochtitlán, the Aztec capital. Before Mexico's independence, Mexico City was the capital of New Spain. The city was captured by U.S. troops during the Mexican War, was later conquered by the French army, and was finally recaptured by Mexican rebel forces during the Mexican Revolution.

Mexico City always surprises visitors with its sophistication and European air. It is a culturally rich, dynamic city full of Aztec ruins, colonial buildings, beautiful parks, superb shopping malls, and excellent museums. On the other hand, some of the poorest Mexicans live in Mexico City. Also, the city has developed a critical pollution problem in recent years. The millions of cars, trucks, and buses swarming the city produce pollutants that are easily trapped in the bowl-shaped valley where Mexico City is.

RELIGION

THE FIRST INDIANS in Mexico were probably hunter-gatherers from Asia who crossed the Bering Strait tens of thousands of years ago. When changes in climate killed off their food source, they were forced to cultivate the land. Agriculture became so important to them that they began worshiping gods whom they believed would provide rain and protect their harvests.

The indigenous Indians worshiped many gods. Each of these gods controlled a different aspect of life and had its own personality, being kind or cruel. Some Indian groups believed that their gods required human sacrifice as a payment for granting them favors, so the Indians built temples to honor the gods.

Above: **Pictures of Catholic saints.**

Opposite: **The image of the Virgin of Guadalupe adorns the facade of the cathedral of the same name.**

ARRIVAL OF CATHOLICISM

After the Spanish conquest, Catholic missionaries came to Mexico from Spain to convert the Indians to Christianity. The missionaries were often sent to remote villages. Converting the Indians was not difficult because of certain similarities between Catholicism and indigenous religions.

Realizing they had a better chance of succeeding if they compromised, the missionaries allowed the Indians to keep some of their own religious traditions. They also built churches on or near Indian temples, often destroying the temples and using the same stones to build the churches. The indigenous population began to worship many Catholic saints as Indian deities, thus creating a new religious system combining Christian and Indian beliefs. In urban areas, Indian culture was eventually overrun by European culture, and indigenous beliefs disappeared.

Early missionaries in Mexico and the colonial government were so persistent in their efforts to convert the indigenous population that Catholic churches and chapels were built in almost every village.

ANTI-CHURCH REFORMS

From the time of the Spanish conquest, the Catholic Church has been regarded with some suspicion by *mestizos* and Indians. Although some early priests tried to protect the Indians, many clergymen exploited the indigenous population. During the War of Independence, the Catholic Church, afraid of losing its power, backed the conservatives. In response, the new government after independence began enacting anti-Catholic laws. Many of these laws were passed during the presidency of Benito Juárez. The Mexican Revolution further restricted the Church.

The Constitution of 1917 contains many reforms that limit the power of the Church. A man and a woman must marry in a civil court before they can have a religious ceremony. Land and buildings that once belonged to the Catholic Church are now state property. No church leader is allowed to make a political statement in public. Priests are not allowed to vote or to wear their clerical robes in public. The government also limits the number of men who can become priests, and these are restricted to local-born Mexicans.

THE VIRGIN OF GUADALUPE

There is a fervent and widespread belief in Mexico in the miracle of the Virgin of Guadalupe.

According to legend, in 1531, a poor Indian named Juan Diego saw the Virgin of Guadalupe on his way to church, one day after he had converted to Catholicism. She appeared as an Indian maiden on Tepeyac Hill at La Villa, just outside Mexico City. She asked Diego to tell the local bishop to build a shrine in her honor on the hill, so that she could protect the Indians. The bishop, however, did not believe Diego's story.

The next day, the Virgin appeared again. When Diego told the bishop about this, he demanded proof. When the Virgin appeared a third time, Diego told her about the bishop's request for proof. She told him to collect roses from a spot on the hill where roses had never grown before. Diego wrapped the roses in a blanket and brought them to the bishop. When he unwrapped the parcel, they both saw the image of the Virgin imprinted on the inside of the blanket. The bishop then built the shrine and placed the cloth in it.

The Basilica of the Virgin of Guadalupe was rebuilt in 1976. The construction was financed by the government, a remarkable gesture considering its official anti-Church stance. The government's involvement in the building of the church indicates the importance of the Virgin to Mexicans. In 1990, Juan Diego was canonized by Pope John Paul II during his visit to Mexico.

Reenacting the crucifixion of Jesus Christ. Many people fast and pray before the celebration of Easter to atone for their sins.

THE CHURCH TODAY

Despite their best efforts, the Spanish missionaries were not able to completely destroy all Indian beliefs. Nature, magic, and mystery remain an important part of indigenous religions. Some Indians living in remote villages still worship their ancestral gods, but most Mexicans practice a form of Catholicism that incorporates elements of Indian faiths.

The Catholic Church has lost much of its influence on the lives of Mexicans. Although 90 percent of Mexicans are Catholic, evangelical groups are increasing rapidly. Currently, 6 percent of the Mexican population is Protestant. Church attendance among Catholics, especially in urban areas, is dropping, as is the ratio of priests to population. Divorce is becoming more socially acceptable, and many people use birth control, which runs against Catholic teachings. Abortion is a fairly common practice, although the Church has successfully blocked efforts to legalize it.

In 1999, Pope John Paul II visited Mexico for the fourth time. The pope was met at the airport by President Ernesto Zedillo and was allowed to wear his clerical robes and celebrate mass in public. Hundreds of

thousands of people flocked to see him. The pope's visits have strengthened relations between the Mexican government and the Catholic Church. Despite the law forbidding non-Mexican priests, there are many foreign priests in Mexico due to the shortage of local-born priests. Though Church leaders do at times publicly speak out against the government, most priests keep a low profile.

While laws restricting the Church's influence used to be strictly enforced, they have become more relaxed today. The voting population is overwhelmingly Catholic, so some political leaders try to get around enforcing the rules to attract more votes.

Although the Church as an institution has weakened over the years, religious beliefs are still an integral part of Mexican life. Village priests are often powerful community leaders, and husband-wife relationships are still based on the teachings of the Bible and the Church.

Crowds of believers are always present at religious celebrations in Mexico.

LANGUAGE

MOST MEXICANS SPEAK SPANISH, the official language of most Latin American countries. In fact, with 101.9 million people, Mexico has the largest Spanish-speaking population in the world. However, there are still many Indians living in remote areas in Mexico who cannot speak Spanish.

MEXICAN SPANISH

The Spanish spoken in Mexico is different from the Spanish spoken in Spain, somewhat the way the English spoken in the United States is different from the English spoken in Britain. Mexican Spanish is a hybrid of Spanish, Indian languages, and some English.

Even within Mexico, there are differences in the way people speak Mexican Spanish. People from the *tierra fría*—the highlands—tend to speak slowly and enunciate every word, while people living in the *tierra caliente*—the tropical zones—speak faster and often drop the ending sound of words, particularly if the words end in the letter "s."

Mexicans prefer to speak indirectly to avoid trouble or commitment. This has led to remarkable creativity in the Mexican use of Spanish. Many words have double meanings that would not be understood by people who are not familiar with the connotations. Excessive frankness or directness is considered rude, and even serious discussions must be preceded by political gossip or small talk about family.

Many words used in English are of Mexican-Spanish origin, such as canyon, corral, desperado, lasso, patio, rodeo, and stampede.

Above: **Mexicans read and write in Spanish.**

Opposite: **The stop sign is translated as** *alto* **in Spanish.**

A classroom in a village school. The Mexican government has set up schools where Spanish is taught to Indian students in an effort to integrate them into mainstream society and help them improve their economic status.

INDIAN LANGUAGES

While millions of Mexican Indians speak their indigenous languages on a daily basis, most are also fluent in Spanish. The most widely spoken Indian language in Mexico is Nahuatl, the language of the Aztecs, followed by the Mixtec, Mayan, Zapotec, and Otomi languages. These languages are different from one another, with very few common words between them.

It is estimated that there are 59 Indian languages in Mexico today, in addition to numerous minor dialects. Some of these dialects are spoken only by a few individuals or groups.

The Spanish thought they could accelerate Indian integration into Mexican society by eliminating indigenous languages. Although attempts by the Spanish to wipe out Indian languages from Mexico were not completely successful, it is estimated that as many as 93 Indian languages have disappeared since the Spanish conquest.

Government policy no longer forces the Spanish language on the Indians. For instance, when the government began a war against illiteracy in 1944, it provided Indians with important information in their own languages, though written in Roman script. These communications enabled the Indians to learn about the merits of learning Spanish. They realized they could improve their education and economic condition by learning Spanish. Television and radio, which broadcast mainly in Spanish, were added incentives for Indians to learn the language. Most Indians have today become part of the Spanish-speaking community, while keeping their distinct culture and traditions.

COMMISSION FOR THE DEFENSE OF SPANISH

The government of Mexico tries very hard to maintain its cultural independence from the United States. In the early 1980s, the government noticed that more and more English words were creeping into the Spanish language. For example, people were calling themselves Charlie instead of Carlos, or Paul instead of Pablo. Owners of restaurants and shops, thinking foreign words fashionable and good for business, began giving their establishments English names, such as Shirley's and Arthur's.

In 1982, the government created the Commission for the Defense of the Spanish Language. The commission's purpose was to prevent English from becoming mixed with the Spanish language. It declared war on the apostrophe—which does not exist in Spanish—as the principal symbol of cultural mixing. The commission also made radio and television commercials that mocked people using English phrases. However, the commission's impact has been slight, and English words from the United States continue to gain currency in Mexico.

HEY AMIGO!

FORMALITIES AND TITLES Mexicans have two ways of saying "you." *Tú* ("too") is the familiar form, used when talking to friends. *Usted* ("oos-TED") is the formal form. Mexicans are very strict about when to use each form. It is considered impolite to use *tú* when greeting a stranger, an elder, or someone of a higher social status. In this case, *tutear* ("too-teh-AHR"), which means "to use the pronoun *tú*," is acceptable only after it has been agreed by both parties to do so.

These typists in Mexico City provide a service to people who either are unable to write or do not have access to a typewriter.

NICKNAMES Nicknames are very common in Mexico and are simply versions of proper names, as in Tonio from Antonio. Many are derived from people's looks, personalities, or jobs. Someone who is overweight may be called *Gordo* ("GOR-doh"), or "fatty," and someone with a big nose might be nicknamed *Chato* ("CHAH-toh"), or "nose." "Junior" is an insulting nickname for those whose status comes from the power or money of their parents.

CLASS DIFFERENCES Although they deny the existence of racial discrimination, many upper-class Mexicans have developed a special vocabulary, which indicates in a subtle way their position in society.

Wealthy Mexicans are called *gente de razón* ("HEN-tay day rah-SOHN"), or "people of reason." The opposite of the *gente de razón* are the *gente indígena* ("een-DEE-hay-nah"), or the Indians. Some *mestizos* call themselves *cristianosas* ("kris-tee-ah-NOH-sahs") to indicate that they are not Indians. The poor, even if they are *mestizo*, are referred to as *indios* ("EEN-dee-ohs") or *inditos* ("een-

DEE-tohs"), which literally means "little Indians." This term is considered an insult.

The use of informal language or slang is common among friends.

SLANG This is an important method of communication in Mexico, which can be difficult to understand for those unfamiliar with it. For example, Mexicans refer to the United States as "the other side." They also call cars "ships," and money "wool."

MALINCHISMO The Mexican word for traitor, or for one who rejects his own cultural heritage in favor of foreign things, is *malinchista* ("mah-leen-CHEES-tah"). It comes from the name of an Indian maiden, La Malinche, one of Hernán Cortés' translators and also his mistress. Through La Malinche and a Spanish translator, Cortés was able to form alliances with Indians that aided the success of the Spanish conquest.

NONVERBAL LANGUAGE

1. *Ojo* ("OH-ho"), or "eye," is a shrewd person's way of warning someone to be careful or to watch out.
2. *¿Quién sabe?* ("KEE-en SAH-bay"), or "Who knows?" is usually accompanied by raised eyebrows, facial contortions, and groans. It means "I take no responsibility."
3. *Las uñas* ("lahs OO-nyas"), or "fingernails," may refer to either a thief or a theft and is often used as a warning that a known thief is nearby or as a way of saying that something has been stolen.
4. This gesture is used to indicate the height of inanimate objects.
5. This gesture is used to indicate the height of animals.
6. This gesture is used to indicate the height of people. (It can be insulting to use gesture 4 or 5 when referring to people.)
7. *Lana* ("LAH-nah"), or "money," is a way of saying something is expensive.
8. *Ijole!* ("ee-HOH-lay"), or "Wow!" The fingers should make an audible pop.
9. *No, ni modos* ("no, nee MOH-dohs"), or "No, no way."
10. *Adelante* ("ad-day-LAHN-tay"), or "ahead," is a common gesture, though it looks confusing. It looks like "go away," but it means "come here" or "move forward."
11. *Momentito, ahoritita* ("moh-men-TEE-toh, ah-or-ree-TEE-tah"), or "a moment," means "not much," "a little bit," or even "I'll be right back." It is often used in place of a verbal promise that one knows cannot be fulfilled.
12. *No, gracias* ("no, GRAH-see-ahs"), or "No, thank you," is used in the same way as in the United States as a sign of appreciation when turning something down.

1

2

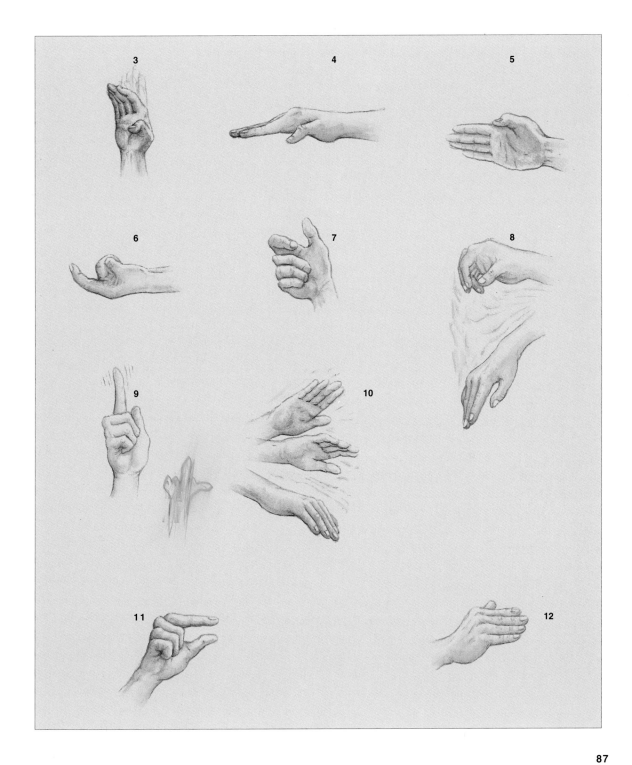

ARTS

MEXICO'S ARTISTIC HERITAGE is one of the oldest and richest in the Americas. The country's artistic history stretches back more than 3,000 years.

Mexican art and architecture display a combination of cultural and social themes, such as the ancient Indian civilizations, Spanish colonialism, Catholicism, and the revolutionary ideas of 19th-century politics in Mexico.

Mexican indigenous art before the Spanish conquest achieved a remarkable level of development and sophistication. Created by Indians with virtually no outside influence, Mexican ancient art is valued not only for its artistic merit, but also for its historical and archaeological importance.

Above: **The blend of Spanish and Indian architectural styles can be seen in the facades of old colonial churches.**

Opposite: **The great city of Tenochtitlán. Artist Diego Rivera's mural reflects Mexico's renewed pride in its ancient heritage.**

Indian groups managed to preserve their art and culture after the arrival of the Spaniards, but European styles gradually influenced Mexican writing, painting, music, and architecture. After the revolution, the country began to use its unique culture to promote a sense of national identity. Art became a powerful medium for patriotism.

Mexican art continues to draw inspiration from the country's colorful history and unique blend of Spanish and indigenous Mexican styles and themes. Nevertheless, in recent years, the artistic traditions of other countries have begun to put their mark in Mexican art, providing new freedoms and inspiration for Mexican artists to develop new techniques.

MEXICAN INDIAN ART AND ARCHITECTURE

Most Mexican indigenous art before the arrival of the Spanish was inspired by religion. The gods of the indigenous Indians dominated every facet of Indian life, and many Indian works of art were created as offerings to the gods. The Olmecs, who developed the first civilized culture in Mexico between 1300 and 400 B.C., were also the country's first artists. They made jewelry and ceramics, but are best known for their stone carvings. Huge shapes of human heads, discovered mostly in the state of Veracruz, are the earliest portraits that remain of these ancient people. These heads are believed to have been created in honor of the Olmec rulers.

The Olmecs built the first pyramid, an architectural style that would become important in every culture that followed. The Olmec pyramids began as mounds of earth covered with rough stones. They were later developed into beautiful, elaborate structures. The pyramids served several functions. They were temples where priests could pray and perform rituals for the gods. They were also symbolic mountains meant to bring people closer to Heaven. The Pyramid of the Niches in Tajín is one of the most magnificent in Mexico.

Later civilizations, such as the Maya, continued to build magnificent cities and pyramids. The Mayan cities of Palenque, Chichén Itzá, and Uxmal display the Mayans' extraordinary artistic talent. The last indigenous Mexican empire, the Aztec, founded a magnificent capital, Tenochtitlán, on the site of present-day Mexico City. Teotihuacán, located to the northeast of Mexico City, is another fine example of an ancient Indian city, with extraordinary pyramids, temples, and roads made for the kings.

The Aztec Sunstone is a remarkable work of art and science. The Sunstone is actually used as a calendar to calculate the number of days in a year.

The Indians considered artistic skill a moral virtue and a way of expressing religious fervor. Their accomplishments are remarkable considering the fact that they did not use iron tools. When the Spaniards arrived, they were impressed by the art and architecture of the Mexican Indians. The Spaniards also believed, however, that much of Mexican Indian art was the work of the devil. The Spaniards melted down gold objects, shattered sacred sculptures, and burned artifacts. Some objects have survived, and they have been safely put on display in museums around the country.

The Pyramid of the Magician in Uxmal was built by the Mayans. No iron tools were used to carve or erect the stones.

POST-REVOLUTION ART

The Revolution of 1910 had a dramatic effect on Mexican art. Artists began using patriotic and political themes in their work and used realistic styles to depict contemporary political conflicts. The Revolution also inspired a group of young painters to search for a style that would incorporate the great art of the indigenous Indians, as they felt that their art should be reflection of the common people in Mexico. These artists specialized in painting large murals in public buildings. Three leaders of the Mexican muralist movement were Diego Rivera, David Siqueiros, and José Orozco. Together, they transformed the art world of their time and place.

Rivera was the founder of the movement. Inspired by indigenous Mexican art and his experiences in Europe, he painted murals dealing with Mexican history and society. Siqueiros was a political activist. He fought in the Revolution of 1910, volunteered to fight in the Spanish Civil War of the 1930s, and took part in labor struggles. Having been imprisoned on several occasions, he made social unrest the focus of his paintings. Orozco is considered the best Mexican muralist of all time. While Rivera and Siqueiros were noted also for their work in easel painting and sculpture, Orozco was at his best painting murals. His work reflects strong political feelings and a search for deep and universal symbols.

MODERN ARCHITECTURE

After trying to wipe out pre-Columbian art forms, the Spanish taught the Indians to use European architectural and building techniques. The result was a new architectural style that combined European and indigenous Indian forms.

The development of modern architecture in Mexico in many ways paralleled that of Mexican painting. Mexican architectural tradition, which began in pre-Spanish times, culminated during the rule of dictator Porfirio Díaz. President Díaz was responsible for building the Palace of Fine Arts and the congress building. During the 1920s, architecture adjusted to the political mood of nationalism. The state constructed large buildings decorated with murals and sculptures. As with painting, Mexican architecture entered a creative period in the 1950s, achieving dramatic and exciting results by blending the colors and shapes of traditional Mexican art with modern styles and techniques imported from abroad.

A bird's eye view of the Palace of Fine Arts. Mexico has many fascinating museums that display its rich ancient history, strong artistic tradition, and cultural diversity.

CRAFTS AND FOLK ARTS

Crafts and folk arts have flourished throughout Mexican history, and despite increased modernization, they still make up a vital part of the nation's life and economy. When Mexicans eat, dress, play, or pray, they use replicas of the crafts used by their ancestors.

The making of contemporary Mexican crafts still follow ancient Indian traditions. As in pre-Spanish Mexico, pottery is a major activity, and much of it is still made by hand, without the use of a wheel. Weaving is still frequently done on a backstrap loom. *Huipils* ("wee-peels"), which are

Local pottery for sale. In some remote areas in Mexico, the art of pottery has changed little since pre-Spanish days.

Local crafts are sold in bustling bazaars and street markets everywhere in Mexico.

long embroidered dresses; long blouses; *quexquemetls* ("KEX-kay-meh-tls"), or ponchos; and capes worn in the past by Indian women are still woven today and worn on special occasions such as weddings and fiestas.

Spanish influence on Mexican crafts has been significant. Wool was unknown in ancient Mexico until sheep were introduced into the Americas. *Serapes* (blankets) and *rebozos* (shawls) and some artistic techniques such as glazing are evidence of Spanish influence.

MUSIC

Music was a very important part of the culture of Mexico's early Indians. They believed that music kept the world in motion and controlled natural phenomena. All Indian ceremonies involved music. Indigenous Mexicans also used music to teach children about their history and traditions.

Indigenous Mexicans played whistles, flutes, percussion instruments, drums, giant conch shells, rattles, trumpets, and notched deer bones. The earliest remaining musical instruments date from about 1500 B.C. and were made of bone, wood, animal hide, or baked clay.

The Spanish *conquistadores* tried to destroy Indian music, which they thought was inspired by the devil. Their efforts failed, partly because Spanish priests found it easier to convert the Indians if they allowed the Indians to transfer the use of traditional ceremonial music from the worship of pagan deities to the honoring of Catholic saints. Indians in some parts of Mexico still play the music of their ancestors.

A popular style of Mexican music is the *norteña* ("nor-TAY-nyah"), which combines the tunes of *corridos* ("coh-REE-dos"), or ballads, with waltzes and polkas. These dances were brought to Mexico by thousands of Eastern European and German immigrants who settled in the country in the mid-1800s.

The musicians most associated with Mexico are the *mariachis* ("mah-ree-AH-chees"). *Mariachi* bands consist of anywhere from three to over a dozen musicians, who wear big *sombreros*, frilly shirts, cowboy boots, and tight dark suits embroidered with silver. They sing romantic, sentimental songs accompanied by guitars and violins. In Mexico City, *mariachi* bands gather at Garibaldi Square, hoping to be hired by passers-by. In Mexican tradition, suitors hire *mariachis* to serenade their lovers, husbands to serenade their wives. The most popular serenading hours are between two and four o'clock in the morning. *Mariachis* are present at virtually all Mexican parties, weddings, and public fiestas.

A strolling *mariachi* band may stop under the windows of an apartment building to serenade prospective clients.

The Feast of the Virgin of Guadalupe. While most of Mexico's traditional dances are religious in origin and purpose, they are often performed at parties and other fun-filled events.

DANCE

To the ancient Mexicans, dance was as important as music. Like music, dance was highly religious. The Aztecs and Mayans danced to communicate with the gods and to bring in luck. They had dances at almost every occasion, such as marriage, war, hunting, and the harvest. To destroy Indian culture, the Spanish conquerors forbade community dancing, but their efforts failed in the end. Today, the Institute of Fine Arts is home to the Ballet Folklórico, the national folkloric dance troupe.

THE *VOLADORES*

Probably the most spectacular of all traditional dances is the *voladores*, or flying pole dance. It is an ancient rain dance that is still performed by the Nahua and Totonac Indians.

Four men wearing feathered costumes are tightly secured by ropes to a 100-foot (30-m) pole. They represent the four seasons. Another man is seated on a small platform on top of the pole, playing an instrument. The four men with ropes drop off the pole and swing around 13 times before they reach the ground. The total number of rotations, which is 52, represents the number of weeks in a year. The *voladores* is still re-enacted in several Mexican villages.

The most beautiful and powerful Mexican dances are of pre-Spanish origin. The deer dance of the Yaqui Indians—the Yaqui Indian Stag Dance—is popular all over Mexico. Originally performed to attract luck in hunting, this dance is now performed at many religious fiestas and ceremonies. This exciting dance depicts the chase and kill of a deer, with all the dancers portraying animals with amazing realism. Another favorite is the Sandunga dance from Tehuantepec, famous for its beautiful music.

One of the few colorful dances introduced after the Spanish conquest is *los moros*, about the war between Moors and Christians in Spain. It is performed at bullfights and other celebrations. Half the dancers dress as Moors, the other half as Christians. *Los moros* may be performed by as large a troupe as a thousand dancers but usually involves a group of about a dozen. It remains a popular ritual dance, especially around the Federal District and central states.

The Mexican hat dance is a national folk dance that has become famous around the world. Dancers clap their hands and step on the rim of the hat as they circle it. Other colorful dances are the Zapotec feather dance from the state of Oaxaca and the Nahua *quetzal* dance from the city of Puebla. *Quetzal* dancers wear feathered headdresses and carry shields.

The National Library in Mexico City.

LITERATURE

Carlos Fuentes (b. 1928) is Mexico's best known contemporary writer. Two of his major novels, *The Death of Artemio Cruz* and *Where the Air is Clear*, portray the upper, and often seamier, side of Mexican society and politics. Both these novels have been translated into foreign languages.

Octavio Paz (b. 1914) is a writer and poet noted for his elegant style, as well as his insight and knowledge of Mexican society. One of his most famous works is *The Labyrinth of Solitude: Life and Thought in Mexico*. In this book, he tries to analyze the Mexican character. In 1990, Paz became the first local-born Mexican to receive the Nobel prize in literature.

A surprising number of well-known British and American authors have written about Mexico or set some of their best novels in Mexico, usually after having lived or traveled there. These authors include Saul Bellow, Ray Bradbury, Graham Greene, Jack Kerouac, D.H. Lawrence, Jack London, Katherine Anne Porter, Oscar Lewis, and John Steinbeck.

THE ART SCENE TODAY

The art scene in contemporary Mexico, in the tradition of its rich history, continues to nurture and churn out a great number of artists. Unfortunately, these artists are hardly known outside Mexico. Although there is some international recognition for Mexican muralists like Diego Rivera, other contemporary artists such as José Fors, Manuel González Serrano, Alicia Rahon, Ricardo Martínez, and José Orozco are largely unknown outside their home country. In spite of the many foreign styles that have influenced Mexican art over the years, indigenous Indian style continues to be the backbone of contemporary Mexican art, as shown in Mexican architecture, jewelry, fashion, and advertising.

Budding artists at work. People around the world have come to appreciate the unique beauty of Mexican art.

LEISURE

ONE'S STATUS IN SOCIETY determines what leisure activities one takes up in Mexico. The upper classes spend their leisure time dining out, traveling, and playing sports at country clubs, much as the wealthy in other countries do. Wealthy Mexicans can easily fly to Houston, Los Angeles, or New York to visit friends or go shopping. Poor Mexicans, on the other hand, must work from dawn to dusk to make a living. For them, fiestas are the only leisure they can afford.

Sunday is the most leisurely day of the week for all Mexicans. It is an important family day. Favorite Sunday time fillers include picnics, family gatherings, going to bullfights, and, in smaller towns, going on dates around the town square.

Opposite: **Diving off the cliffs at Acapulco.**

Left: **Many young people and families enjoy going to amusement parks.**

The grand Plaza de Toros in Mexico City is the largest bullfighting arena in the world.

THE BULLFIGHT

Bullfighting was introduced to Mexico by the Spaniards shortly after the conquest. For the next 300 years of colonial rule, bullfights were held regularly in Mexico to commemorate religious and civic celebrations. Bullfighting is one of the country's most popular spectator activities. Mexico City's bullfighting ring, the Plaza de Toros, seats up to 50,000 people. It is the largest bullfighting ring in the world, and twice as large as most rings in Spain.

Bullfighting, while often called a sport, is really more of an art form. It challenges a matador to have control over his own fears, to overcome the bull's ferocity, and to satisfy the expectations of the crowd.

The object of a bullfight is for the matador to kill an untamed bull with a sword. He attempts to do this by following a ritual that has been developed over centuries. The matador is assisted by two mounted *picadores* ("pee-cah-DOH-rehs") and three *banderilleros* ("BUN-derr-ill-YEH-ros"), capemen on foot.

The fight begins when the ring *presidente* ("preh-see-DEN-tay") waves his handkerchief and the first bull rushes in. The average bull weighs about 1,100 pounds (500 kg). Sometimes, dirt is thrown onto its back, so that when it runs, the dirt flying off its back will show off the quickness of its movements. A bullfight is divided into three parts called *tercios* ("TEHR-see-ohs"). The first *tercio* is called *puyazos* ("poo-YAH-sohs"), or stabs. Two *picadores* use lances to weaken the bull's shoulder muscles, causing its head to sag downward. This helps to expose the entry point for the sword's thrust. When the *picadores* leave, the bull is raging but weakened. The second *tercio* involves the *banderilleros*, who sting the bull with lances and barbed sticks. The bull, bleeding profusely, is furious and begins to charge. In the final *tercio*, the matador has 16 minutes to kill the bull, or the fight is over. He attempts to do this by making daring passes at the bull with his cape, or *muleta* ("muh-LEH-tah"), before thrusting his sword between the animal's shoulder blades into its heart.

The *picadores* lance the bull to weaken and enrage it before its final showdown with the matador.

OTHER SPORTS

Despite the popularity of bullfighting, the biggest spectator sport in Mexico is *fútbol* ("FOOT-bohl"), or soccer. The new Azteca Stadium in Mexico City seats up to 100,000 people, twice as many as the Plaza de Toros bullfighting ring. Matches are played in summer and the fall, on Sunday afternoons and Thursday evenings.

Along the Pacific coast and in the southeast, including the Yucatán Peninsula, baseball is extremely popular. Children play in school and after-school leagues, and men play in parks and other open spaces. Mexico has two major baseball leagues.

Training in the Japanese martial art of *karate*. Mexicans enjoy a variety of sports.

Jai alai ("HI ah-LIE") is a game of Spanish-Basque origin similar to handball. It is played by either two or four persons on a three-walled court with a hard rubber ball the size of a golfball. A player hurls the ball against the wall and his opponent tries to catch it in his racket and return it. *Jai alai* is sometimes called *pelota vasca* ("pay-LOH-tah VAS-kah"), or Basque Ball. Cockfighting, which is illegal in the United States, Canada, and many other countries, is a popular Mexican sport. These fights take place in an enclosed pit, usually outdoors. Spectators place bets on their favorite gamecocks. At the start of the fight, handlers hold the birds and allow them to peck at each other just out of range. When the birds become angry, they are released and allowed to engage in a full-out battle, until one is dead.

Blessed with beautiful beaches on both the eastern and western coast, Mexicans take every opportunity to enjoy the sun, sand, and sea.

THE CHARROS

Mexico's only truly national sport is perhaps the *charrería* ("char-reh-REE-ah"), which is similar to the American rodeo. The men who participate are called *charros* ("CHAR-ros") and are considered some of the bravest, strongest men in Mexico.

The skills displayed during a *charrería*—roping, tying, riding, and branding cattle—were developed for use in cattle ranching. These skills also made the *charros* excellent cavalrymen in Mexico's various wars. The *charros* captured enemies and their cannons by lassoing them as if they were cattle.

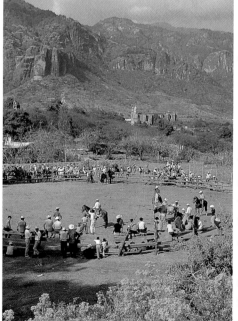

A *charrería* or rodeo during a village festival.

After the Revolution, most large cattle ranches in Mexico were broken up by the government, and the glory days of the *charros* reached an end. In order to continue to compete and show off their skills, the *charros* started the *charrerías*. The biggest *charro* ("CHAR-roh") rings, called *lienzo charros* ("lee-EN-soh CHAR-ros"), are in Mexico City and Guadalajara. Weekly competitions are held on Sundays.

At the start of the show, the horsemen ride around the ring to salute the judges and the public. The first event, called *cala de caballo* ("KAH-lah day kah-BUY-yoh"), is meant to demonstrate the rider's control over the horse. The rider guides his horse through a series of difficult maneuvers.

The second event is called the *coleadero* ("koh-leh-ah-DAY-roh"). The *charro* must grab a wild bull by the tail and roll it over on its back. Points are given for how quickly and neatly the *charro* completes this difficult

task. The remaining events involve bronco bucking, bull riding, and lassoing. Some of these events are the most exciting of the whole show. Women also compete in their own events at the *charrería*. Though they ride their horses sidesaddle as a mark of femininity, they are extremely skilled riders.

Charros give much thought to their clothing and often spend a lot of money on their outfits or on equipment for their horses. The typical *charro* dress includes embroidered shirts, *serapes,* and dark blue pantaloons embroidered in gold.

Charros are famous ladies' men. They idolize women and can be very romantic, and their strength and bravery make them very attractive to women. They are also very devoted to their horses. There is an aura of nostalgia about the *charro*—the hero of a romantic era that is quickly vanishing from contemporary Mexican society.

Besides attaining horsemanship skills, *charros* also learn to use the lasso.

FESTIVALS

MEXICO CELEBRATES MORE FESTIVALS than any other Latin American country. Even before the Spanish arrived, indigenous Mexicans held feasts to celebrate natural phenomena and religious rituals.

FIESTAS

Ancient Indian fiestas were mostly somber religious events. At some of the celebrations, the Indians ate human flesh they had offered as a sacrifice to the gods. Today, while some fiestas are solemn affairs meant to pay homage to a saint, hero, or tradition, many other fiestas are joyful, fun-filled events.

Despite centuries of effort by the Spanish settlers to eradicate pagan rituals and replace them with Christian feasts, many of the original pagan holidays are still celebrated. As a result, on any day of the year, a fiesta is held in at least one town in Mexico.

Fiestas usually last one or two days, but if the patron saint is especially important, they can last up to a week. The Feria de San Marcos is celebrated in Aguascalientes for 10 days every year, starting on Saint Mark's Day on April 25. Festivities are usually held around the church and the main plaza, or *zócalo* ("SOH-kah-loh"), both of which are colorfully decorated. During the day, people crowd the open-air markets to buy candy, fruit, toys, and handicrafts. At night, festivities include folk dances, fireworks, and music. The festivities are usually paid for by someone chosen by the community. It is considered an honor to be chosen, and the sponsor gains the gratitude of the townspeople and a good reputation in the community.

Above: **Chili-red masks of the devil. Many festivities in Mexico celebrate a religious event.**

Opposite: **Fiestas feature ethnic dances and folk music.**

CALENDAR OF EVENTS

Mexican author Octavio Paz wrote that Mexico's poverty, "… can be measured by the frequency and luxuriousness of our holidays. Wealthy countries have very few: there is neither the time nor the desire for them, and they are not necessary … But how could a poor Mexican live without the two or three annual fiestas that make up for his poverty and misery? Fiestas are our only luxury." Some of Mexico's more important holidays are:

January 1	New Year's Day
February 5	Constitution Day
March 21	Birthday of Benito Juárez
May 1	Labor Day
September 16	Independence Day
November 20	Anniversary of the Mexican Revolution
December 25	Christmas

The following are not national holidays but are widely observed and celebrated:

Late February	Carnival
Before Easter	Holy Week
May 5	Anniversary of the Battle of Puebla in 1862
May 10	Mother's Day
July 25	Day of St. James
August 15	Day of the Virgen de la Asunción
August 25	Day of San Luis
September 1	President's annual report to the nation
October 12	Día de la Raza (Day of Ethnicity)
November 2	Day of the Dead (All Soul's Day)
November 22	Day of St. Cecilia
December 12	Feast of Our Lady of Guadalupe, patron saint of Mexico

Mexican families take part in Independence Day celebrations by watching a parade on the streets of Ciudad Juárez.

INDEPENDENCE DAY

The most important Mexican patriotic fiesta is celebrated on September 16, the anniversary of the day in 1810 when Father Miguel Hidalgo proclaimed Mexico's independence from Spain.

This annual celebration begins on September 15 with a reenactment of Father Hidalgo's call to battle, called *El Grito de Dolores*. The ceremony takes place simultaneously throughout Mexico at 11 P.M.

In an internationally televised live broadcast, the president of Mexico appears on the central balcony of the National Palace in Mexico City and repeats the 1810 rallying cry of Father Hidalgo. A replica of the Dolores church bell used to call the battle is then rung, followed by the ringing of the Metropolitan Cathedral bells.

The *zócalo* below the president is filled with celebrating Mexicans, in

Father Miguel Hidalgo, the father of Mexican independence.

the same way that Times Square in New York City is crowded on New Year's Eve. In every municipality in Mexico the same ceremony takes place, with the mayor coming out on the central balcony of the city or town hall, reciting *El Grito* and ringing a replica of the bell of Dolores. In Mexico City and the provinces, magnificent fireworks follow.

El Grito is also recited in the United States in cities where large communities of Mexican-Americans live. Top ministers are sent to cities like Los Angeles, San Francisco, San Diego, Chicago, and New York City to recite the battle cry and give a speech in Spanish next to city officials. Outside Mexico City, bullfights are staged, but this anniversary is usually dedicated to rest. Mexico celebrates the birth of José María Morelos, the hero of the independence, on September 30.

Families gather at the cemetery to welcome back the souls of their departed loved ones.

Food for the dead is placed on a decorated table that includes a photograph of the deceased along with flowers and other offerings.

DAY OF THE DEAD

The Day of the Dead, the most important religious and Indian festival of the year in Mexico, is also one of the most peculiar of all Mexican fiestas. This celebration originated in Europe in the ninth century and was introduced in Mexico by the Spaniards. It blended with existing Aztec beliefs concerning death and departed spirits. Weeks before the event, markets and bakeries sell special breads baked in human form, skull-shaped sweets, toy coffins, and papier-mâché skeletons. Flower markets overflow with marigolds, which in Aztec times were offered to the dead.

On October 31, villagers await the *muertitos chicos* ("moo-ehr-TEE-tohs CHEE-kohs"), or souls of dead children. Toy-shaped cakes, hot chocolate, and honey are offered to sweeten the visit of these souls to earth. Adult souls are believed to return the following night. Families prepare delicious traditional feasts for their arrival. The dead are believed to eat the "spirit" of the food. The next day is the official Day of the Dead. Everyone celebrates by eating the offered food. Often an all-night candlelight vigil is kept in the town cemetery the night the souls are expected to arrive. Families gather on the graves of their departed to keep them company on their annual return.

FEAST OF OUR LADY OF GUADALUPE

Every year on December 12, Mexicans honor the Virgin of Guadalupe to celebrate the day of her miraculous appearance to the Indian peasant Juan Diego. Millions make a pilgrimage to the Basílica de la Virgen to thank her for answered prayers. Many crawl up the hill on their hands and knees, hurting themselves as an act of penitence. In spite of these sacrifices, a festive atmosphere prevails around the church.

Beginning the evening of December 11, the square in front of the Basílica becomes a stage for a night of traditional song and dance. Because this feast is close to Christmas, many Christmas activities also take place. While the largest celebration is held at the shrine outside Mexico City, many smaller celebrations take place in churches throughout Mexico. This shrine is visited by more pilgrims than any other Catholic site in the world, with the exception of the Vatican in Rome.

A celebration in honor of the Virgin of Guadalupe. About six million believers visit the Basílica de la Virgen each year.

THE CHRISTMAS SEASON

The Christmas season in Mexico is a combination of Spanish colonial customs and traditions picked up from the United States.

The *posada* ("poh-SAH-dah"), literally "inn," dates from colonial times, when missionaries tried to illustrate the Christmas story for their Indian converts. Beginning on December 16 and continuing every night through Christmas Eve, *posadas* reenact Joseph and Mary's search for lodging in Bethlehem. Processions move through the streets carrying lighted candles. At the door of a designated house, the group stops, sings traditional *posada* songs, and asks for lodging. After repeated rejections, the door is finally opened. The group joyfully enters and the party begins.

Highlighting the *posada* are traditional food and drink, and for the children, the breaking of the *piñata* ("pee-NYAH-tah"). A *piñata* is a clay pot that is shaped like an animal or a Carnival figure and covered with papier-mâché and ribbons.

In most homes, *piñatas* are filled with candies and toys; some are filled with money. Blindfolded children take turns swinging a broomstick at the *piñata*, which hangs above them on a rope. When the *piñata* shatters, the children scramble for the gifts.

While some Mexican families have adopted the U.S. tradition of giving gifts on Christmas Day, Epiphany on January 6 is the traditional gift-giving day in Mexico.

Epiphany is the day the three gift-bearing kings of the East visited the baby Jesus. Commemorating their arrival in Bethlehem,

During the Christmas season, markets sell candy, sugared fruits, religious figurines, lanterns, toys, masks, dolls, and *piñatas*.

Visiting Santa and his toy factory at Christmas.

Mexican boys playing the part of the three kings wear fake beards, crowns, and long robes and sit in the plazas of towns where children go to have their pictures taken.

For Christmas parties, a special doughnut-shaped cake is baked with a small doll inside. Traditionally, the guest who receives the slice of cake containing the doll must give a feast on February 2.

New Year's celebrations in Mexico used to be similar to Thanksgiving celebrations in the United States; they were traditionally quiet family affairs. Mexico's New Year has since become much like New Year's celebrations in the United States, with lively parties and festivities.

FOOD

MEXICAN CUISINE IS A MELTING POT of flavors, using ingredients and cooking methods from many countries. Spanish cuisine, incorporating some Arabian dishes, brought to Mexico onions, garlic, sugar, beef, pork, chicken, and cheese. Catholic nuns were among the first to mix local food products with those from Spain, creating a unique Mexican taste.

French cuisine was introduced in Mexico during the reign of Maximilian. Breads with that typically French crisp crust and many kinds of sweet rolls can be

Above: **Mexican sweets.**

Opposite: **No Mexican meal is complete without** *tortillas.* **Tortillas are sold in every restaurant and street stall in Mexico.**

found everywhere in Mexico. Flan, an egg custard topped with a layer of caramel, is a French dessert that appears on the menus of almost every Mexican restaurant, both in Mexico and beyond.

Other European contributions to Mexican cuisine include sausages, honey, and beer from Germany and pasta from Italy. Spices and mangos arrived aboard ships from Asia. Hamburgers, doughnuts, pancakes, and pies from the United States are also becoming increasingly popular items on the Mexican menu.

Many foods consumed by people all over the world today originated in Mexico and were introduced to the rest of the world by Spanish *conquistadores* returning home in the 16th century. Corn is probably Mexico's greatest contribution to "international" cuisine; the country has also introduced tomatoes, chocolate, vanilla, various types of squash including pumpkins, peanuts, assorted beans, avocados, chilies, guava, coconuts, pineapples, papayas, and turkeys.

STAPLES: CORN TO TORTILLAS

Ancient Mexican civilizations introduced to the world two priceless foods: corn and chilies. Although many other foods are indigenous to Mexico, these two products remain the main staples of the Mexican diet.

For thousands of years before Cortés arrived in Mexico, corn was the most important food of the indigenous population. The Indians called it *toconayo* ("toh-koh-NAH-yoh"), which means "our meat." They believed that the gods had molded humans from corn.

The Mexicans were known for a time as the "people of corn." All ancient Mexican civilizations devoted ceremonies to gods and goddesses of corn. Although religion in modern Mexico has discontinued this

In the villages, *tortillas* are still made the traditional way—by grinding the corn and mixing it into paste. It is then cooked over a mud-baked oven.

122

CHILI

Chili, an indigenous Mexican food, plays an important part in the country's cuisine. The Aztecs and Mayans, who cultivated and consumed chili, created recipes that are still in use. These ancient peoples believed that chili had medicinal value, and modern nutritionists agree. A fresh chili is an excellent source of vitamin C and minerals. There are over 100 types of chili in Mexico, mostly because of climatic variation within the country. Each chili variety has its own flavor. Generally, the smaller the chili, the hotter it is.

practice, Mexicans continue to revere this ancient food. For example, roadworkers clearing brush from the shoulders of the highway and groundskeepers in public parks rarely cut stalks of wild corn. As a result, it is not unusual to see corn growing in a downtown plaza or in the middle of a construction site.

No part of the corn plant goes unused. The young, tender ears and husks are used for *tamales* ("tah-MAH-lays") and *atole* ("ah-TOH-lay"), and the corn silk is made into a medicinal tea, said to be good for the kidneys. When dried, the kernels are used for *masa* ("MAH-sah") or tortilla dough, the husks for *tamales,* and the dried stalks for cattle feed. Corn is used in everything from popcorn to cornflakes. It is an ingredient in syrups, desserts, corn starch, oil, grits, coloring for caramel, dextrin, glucose flour, and beer and is a feed for poultry and livestock.

The most important use of corn is centuries old. Corn forms *masa*, the dough for tortillas and *tamales*. A Mexican table without tortillas is said to be an empty table, so cornmeal tortillas must be served with every meal. Corn is the basis of hundreds of dishes. The first cooking lesson a peasant's daughter learns is how to prepare the *nixtamal* ("neex-tah-MAHL")—corn cooked in a solution of lime and water—for the next day's tortillas.

Moles and *tamales. Mole* is a very rich sauce made from more than 30 ingredients, all of which are ground or puréed. A good *mole* sauce takes two days to prepare.

TRADITIONAL MEALS

Mexico's best-known traditional foods include *tacos* ("TAH-kohs"); *enchiladas* ("en-chee-LAH-dahs"); *tamales*, cornmeal dough filled with meat and chili sauce and wrapped in cornhusks and steamed; *quesadillas* ("kay-sah-DEE-yahs"), grilled or fried *tortillas* stuffed with meat, cheese, potatoes, squash blossoms, or chilies; *chalupas* ("chah-LOO-pahs"), tortillas fried and topped with meat and beans, chilies, tomatoes, and onions; *gorditas* ("gor-DEE-tahs"), small, thick tortillas fried with chopped meat and vegetables, cheese, shredded lettuce, and chili sauce on top; and *flautas* ("FLAH-oo-tahs"), extra-long tacos.

Another famous Mexican dish is *chiles rellenos* ("CHEE-lehs reh-lee-EH-nos"). Tangy, delicious, long green peppers are stuffed with either cheese or ground meat, dipped in egg batter, fried, and then simmered in a bland tomato sauce.

For a two-month period beginning in mid-August, a special dish called *chile en nogada* ("CHEE-lee en noh-GAH-dah") is served. The stuffing is often made from ground pork, and the chilis are decorated with sauce, seeds, and parsley to make the red, white, and green colors of the Mexican flag. This dish is served to celebrate Mexican Independence Day.

Water flavored with fruit juice is very popular in Mexico. Soft drinks are another favorite.

TRADITIONAL DRINKS

Mexicans are great coffee drinkers, especially since high quality coffee is grown in Mexico. Coffee is always served at the end of a meal, never before, as most Mexicans prefer not to drink coffee on an empty stomach. Because Mexican coffee is very strong, it is almost always served with a lot of sugar. A popular coffee drink is *café con leche* ("kah-FEH kon LAY-chay"), a blend of strong black coffee and hot milk frequently served in a tall, thick glass.

Hot chocolate has been consumed in Mexico since pre-Spanish times. It is a favorite drink for modern Mexicans at both breakfast and supper. Mexicans drink hot chocolate with a touch of cinnamon, a custom dating back to the ancient Aztecs, who added honey and cinnamon instead of sugar. Not surprisingly, Mexicans also drink corn. *Masa,* the dough used to make tortillas, is the foundation for *atole* ("ah-TOH-lay"), a widely-enjoyed beverage prepared by diluting *masa* in water and boiling it until it is as thick as a milkshake. Mexicans make a good number of alcoholic beverages from fruits or cacti. Tequila, *mescal* ("mays-KAHL"), and *pulque* ("POOL-kay") are all made from the agave plant. Some drinks, such as tequila, are famous around the world.

Mexican fast food.

MARKETS AND FOOD STALLS

Mexicans shop daily at open markets for fresh food. There are temporary and permanent markets. They are the best places to go to for fresh fruit and vegetables. Bartering, or trading goods, is common and even expected in most marketplaces.

Tiendas ("tee-EN-dahs") are small grocery stores. In some smaller towns and villages, these stores also serve as social centers. *Conasupos* ("koh-nah-SOO-pohs") are government-owned stores originally designed to sell basic staples at controlled prices. The government dispatches mobile *conasupos,* usually a large truck or trailer, to remote areas of the country where no permanent stores are found. Prices are usually lower at *conasupos* than at other stores.

Finally, there are the *supermercados* ("soo-per-mer-KAH-dos"), which can vary from large *tiendas* to warehouse-size stores. Prices are usually high at the *supermercados,* but shoppers have a broader selection of products. *Fondas* ("FOHN-dahs") are food stalls found in the markets that sell meals, including beans, rice, soup, and tortillas. Sidewalk stands, where fastfood is sold, are also popular.

126

REFRIED BEAN DIP

1 can spicy refried beans
1 chopped medium onion
1 bunch green onions, chopped
4–8 ounces (113–226 g) grated cheddar cheese
8 ounces (226 g) sour cream
2 chopped tomatoes

1. Heat beans and chopped onion in a pan, adding a little water to make the mixture smooth. Allow to cool.
2. Spread bean mixture onto a large flat plate.
3. Spread sour cream on beans.
4. Sprinkle chopped tomatoes, cheese, and green onions on sour cream.
5. Chill in refrigerator for one hour. Serve with potato chips, corn chips, or nachos.

MEALTIMES

Mexicans start their mornings with a light breakfast, served between 6 and 8 A.M. The first meal of the day usually consists of coffee with *tamales* or a piece of bread or pastry. Brunch is a heartier meal. Eggs with meat or tortillas, accompanied by coffee and milk or fresh fruit juices, are served between 11 A.M. and noon.

The Mexican midday meal, *la comida* ("lah koh-MEE-dah"), is the heaviest and most traditional meal of the day. It is usually not served until around 2 or 3 P.M. The *comida* may include soup, rice or pasta, beans, tortillas or bread, dessert, and a fruit juice or beer. After lunch, nearly everything and everyone shuts down for the *siesta*.

Between 7 and 8 P.M., Mexicans enjoy their own form of English high tea called the *merienda* ("may-ree-EN-dah"). It consists of a cup of hot chocolate, coffee, or *atole*, and some pastries and *tamales*.

Cena ("SAY-nah"), or dinner, is the third major meal of the day. It can be served anytime between 7.30 P.M. and midnight, but is usually eaten between 9 and 10 P.M. It is lighter than *la comida* and might include leftovers from lunch, such as *tacos* or tortillas.

THE MEXICAN KITCHEN

While many kitchens in Mexico have modern utensils and appliances, such as blenders and food processors, many essential cooking tools used in modern Mexico were created thousands of years ago. Mexicans rely extensively on clay cookware, bowls, and pitchers. The following are some traditional Mexican cooking tools:

BEAN MASHER This is usually made from wood.

MOLINILLO This is a beautifully-carved chocolate beater, usually made from wood.

COMAL This is a round, flat plate of tin or unglazed earthenware on which tortillas are cooked.

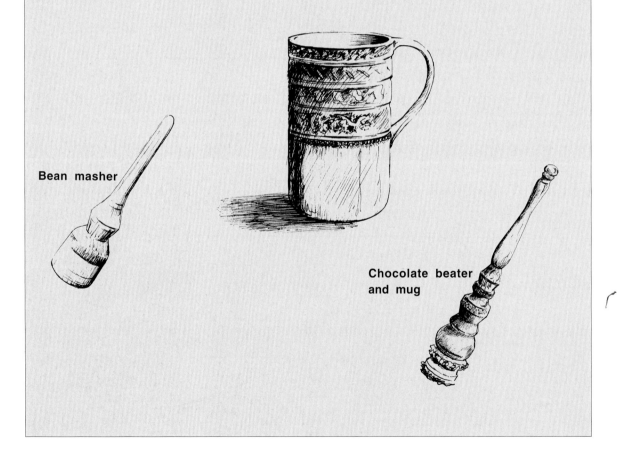

Bean masher

Chocolate beater
and mug

FLAN MOLD This is a three-piece tin utensil for oven-cooking flan in a water bath.

METATE This is a sloping, rectangular piece of volcanic rock, supported on three stout legs. Together with a *metlapil*, or stone rolling pin, it is used for grinding corn, chilies, *cacao*, and other ingredients for making sauces.

MOLCAJETE AND TEJOLATE These are the parts of a mortar made from porous, volcanic stone and pestle. They are used to grind spices and make sauces and are considered indispensable in a Mexican kitchen.

CHIQUIHUITE This is the traditional tortilla basket made from woven reed grass and lined with a cloth to keep the tortillas warm.

TORTILLA PRESS This is used for rolling and shaping tortillas.

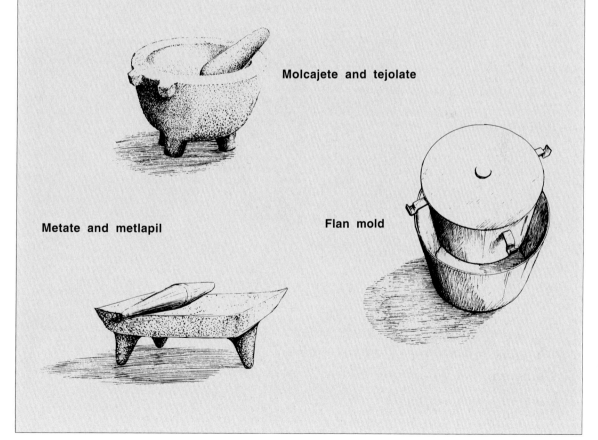

Molcajete and tejolate

Metate and metlapil

Flan mold

ZUCCHINI AND CORN CASSEROLE

This recipe serves four.

2 tablespoons butter or margarine

1 chopped large onion

1 green bell pepper, cored,
   seeded, and chopped

1$\frac{1}{2}$ pounds (680 g) sliced zucchini

2 cups (500 ml) frozen whole-kernel corn

2 large ripe tomatoes cut into chunks

2 chopped tomatoes

4 tablespoons water

Salt and pepper

Preheat oven to 350°F (176°C). Melt butter or margarine in a Dutch oven or heavy pan over medium heat. Add onion and bell pepper and cook for 5–7 minutes, stirring until soft. Add zucchini. Stir until vegetables are coated with butter or margarine. Turn off heat. Add corn, tomatoes, and water. Add salt and pepper to taste. Stir vegetables using a long-handled wooden spoon. Cover the Dutch oven or heavy pan and place in the oven. Cook for 20 minutes.

Wearing oven mitts, remove the Dutch oven from the oven and place on the stovetop. Remove the lid and pierce the zucchini with a knife to check that they are tender. If it is not, place the lid back on the Dutch oven, return it to the oven, and cook for 5 more minutes. Add salt and pepper to taste. Serve hot.

CHICKEN WITH MOLE SAUCE

This recipe serves four.

1 chicken, cut into 8 serving pieces
1 quartered onion
4 cloves garlic, peeled and halved
6 sprigs each of fresh thyme, oregano,
    and parsley
12 small chilis
3 peeled ripe tomatoes
$^1/_4$ cup (312 ml) sesame seeds
1 tablespoon dried oregano

1 clove
1 teaspoon ground allspice
$^1/_4$ cup (62 ml) vegetable oil
1 quartered small onion
8 cloves of garlic, peeled
1–2-inch (3–5-cm) piece of cinnamon stick
1 peeled and chopped plantain
1 ounce (28 g) unsweetened chocolate
Salt to taste

Place chicken in a stew pot and add onion, garlic, and fresh herbs. Cover with water and bring to a boil. Cover the pot and simmer for about 30 minutes until chicken is tender. Remove the stems from the chilis, cut in half lengthwise, and remove seeds. Toast chilis briefly in a hot skillet, but do not overcook. Place chilis in a small bowl, cover with hot water, and set aside. Place the peeled tomatoes in a blender and pulse a few times. Toast sesame seeds in the skillet and add to the blender along with dried oregano, clove, and allspice. Blend until smooth. Add oil to the skillet and fry onion for about 5 minutes. Add garlic cloves and cinnamon stick and fry for 2–3 minutes. Remove with a slotted spoon and put in the blender. Fry plantain for a few minutes and add to the blender along with chilis and water. Blend everything until smooth. Strain the sauce and return to the skillet. Add chocolate and season with salt. Add 2 cups (500 ml) of the chicken broth to the skillet along with the stewed chicken pieces. Cook for another 20–25 minutes uncovered. The sauce should be fairly thick when served. Serve hot with rice or soft tortillas.

A   **B**   **C**   **D**   **E**

1

Tijuana

Ensenada

BAJA
CALIFORNIA
NORTE

*GUADALUPE
ISLAND*

SONORA

Sonora Desert

Ciudad
Juarez

UNITED STATES OF AMERIC

Hermosillo

CHIHUAHUA

Chihuahua

Rio Bravo de

2

Gulf of California

BAJA
CALIFORNIA
SUR

Ciudad Obregón

Yaqui

Fuerte

Sierra Madre

COAHUILA

Norte

NUEVO
LEÓN

Matamoros

G u

La Paz

SINALOA

DURANGO

Torreón

Monterrey

TAMAULIPAS

3

Mazatlán

Victoria
de Durango

ZACATECAS

SAN LUIS
POTOSÍ

Gulf Coastal Plain

Sierra Madre Oriental

Tampico

*P
A
C
I
F
I
C*

Rio Grande de Santiago

NAYARIT

AGUASCA-
LIENTES

San Luis
Potosí

Puerto Vallarta

Guadalajara

Yerbabuena

JALISCO

León

GUANA-
JUATO

QUERÉ-
TARO

HIDALGO

Dolores

Tula

Texcoco
Lake

Tuxpan

Tajín

Gulf of Campeche

*ISLAS DE
REVILLAGIGEDO*

*Colima
(14,236 ft/
4,339 m)*

Periçutín
*(17,426 ft/
5,311 m)*

MEXICO CITY

Ixtaccíhuatl
(17,265 ft/ 5,268 m)

VERACRUZ

CAMP

4

COLIMA

Manzanillo

MICHOACÁN

Popocatépetl
(17,828 ft/5,454 m)

MORELOS

Puebla

PUEBLA

Veracruz

Coatzacoalcos

TABASCO

Balsas

Michoacán

*Isthmus
of
Tehuantepec*

Pale

GUERRERO

OAXACA

CHI

Acapulco

Monte Albán

Oaxaca

San
Cristóbal
de las
Casas

*O
C
E
A
N*

● Capital city
• Major town
▲ Mountain Peak
■ Ancient Site

Height of land (feet)

over 16,000
9,000 - 16,000
6,000 - 9,000
3,000 - 6,000
1,500 - 3,000
600 - 1,500
0 - 600

N

5

MAP OF MEXICO

Acapulco, D4
Aguascalientes, C3

Baja California Norte, A1–A2
Baja California Sur, A2–B3

Campeche, E4–F4
Cancún, F3
Chiapas, E4–E5
Chihuahua, B1–C2
Ciudad Juarez, C1
Coahuila, C2–C3
Colima, C4
Cozumel Island, F3–F4

Distrito Federal, C4–D4
Durango, B2–C3

Guadalajara, C4
Guanajuato, C3–D4
Guerrero, C4–D5

Hermosillo, B2
Hidalgo, D4

Jalisco, C3–C4

Manzanillo, C4
Mazatlán, B3
Mexico City, C4–D4
Michoacán, C4–D4
Monterrey, D3
Morelos, D4

Nayarit, C3–C4
Nuevo León, C2–D3

Oaxaca, D4–E5

Puebla, D4
Puerto Vallarta, C4

Querétaro, D3–D4
Quintana Roo, F3–F4

San Cristóbal de las Casas, E4
San Luis Potosí, C3–D4
Sinaloa, B2–C3
Sonora, A1–B2

Tabasco, E4
Tajín, D4
Tamaulipas, D2–D3
Tampico, D3
Tijuana, A1
Torreón, C3
Tula, D4
Tuxpan, D4

Veracruz, D3–E4

Yucatán, E3–F4

Zacatecas, C3

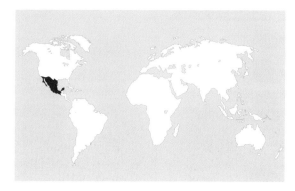

F

f Mexico

Tropic of Cancer

Mérida
Cancún
YUCATÁN
Cozumel Island
Yucatan Peninsula
QUÍNTANA ROO

BELIZE

GUATEMALA
HONDURAS
EL SALVADOR

ECONOMIC MEXICO

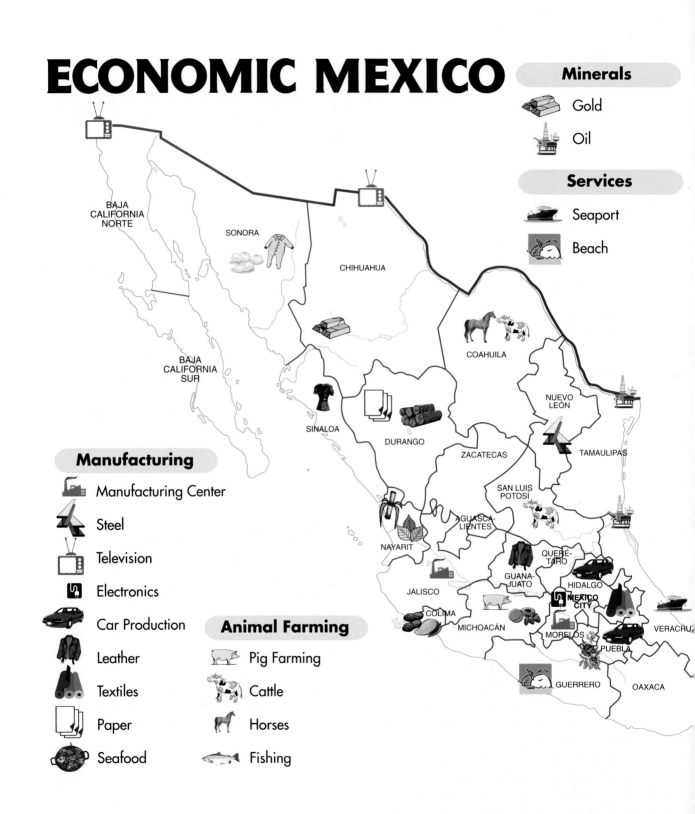

Minerals
- Gold
- Oil

Services
- Seaport
- Beach

Manufacturing
- Manufacturing Center
- Steel
- Television
- Electronics
- Car Production
- Leather
- Textiles
- Paper
- Seafood

Animal Farming
- Pig Farming
- Cattle
- Horses
- Fishing

BAJA CALIFORNIA NORTE

BAJA CALIFORNIA SUR

SONORA

CHIHUAHUA

COAHUILA

NUEVO LEÓN

TAMAULIPAS

SINALOA

DURANGO

ZACATECAS

SAN LUIS POTOSÍ

AGUASCA-LIENTES

NAYARIT

QUERÉ-TARO

GUANA-JUATO

HIDALGO

JALISCO

MEXICO CITY

COLIMA

MICHOACÁN

MORELOS

VERACRUZ

PUEBLA

GUERRERO

OAXACA

Agriculture

 Coffee

 Oranges

 Mangoes

 Bananas

 Sugar Cane

 Tobacco

 Soybeans

 Cotton

 Peanuts

 Rice

 Flowers

 Tropical Fruits

 Logging

ABOUT THE ECONOMY

OVERVIEW
Mexico's free market economy is made up of a combination of modern and traditional industry and agriculture. Mexico has doubled its trade with the United States and Canada since it became a member of NAFTA in 1994.

GDP
US$484 billion (1999)

GDP PER CAPITA
US$4,974 (1999)

GDP SECTORS
Agriculture: 5%
Industry: 29%
Services: 66% (1999)

CURRENCY
1 peso = 100 centavos
US$1 = 9 New Pesos (Aug. 2001)

MAJOR EXPORTS
Agricultural products: avocados, beans, coffee, corn, cotton, fruit, oilseeds, sugarcane, winter vegetables
Minerals: copper, gold, lead, natural gas, oil, silver, zinc
Manufactured goods: cars, clothing, electronics, oil products, textiles

MAJOR IMPORTS
Aircrafts, car parts for assembly, heavy machinery for agriculture, metal working, steel industries

MAJOR TRADING PARTNERS
Brazil, Canada, Chile, China, Germany, Italy, Japan, South Korea, United Kingdom, United States, Venezuela

TOURISM
19.4 million tourists (1997)

WORKFORCE
Trade and Services: 55%
Industry: 21%
Agriculture, forestry, and fishing: 24% (1997)

UNEMPLOYMENT RATE
2.7% (1999)

COMMUNICATIONS
Telephone lines: 9.6 million (1998)
Internet users: 2.5 million (2000)
Internet Service Providers: 51 (2000)

TRANSPORTATION
Airports: 1,848 (2000)
Highways: 201,319 miles (323,977 km) (1999)
Railways: 19,293 miles (31,048 km) (1998)

CULTURAL MEXICO

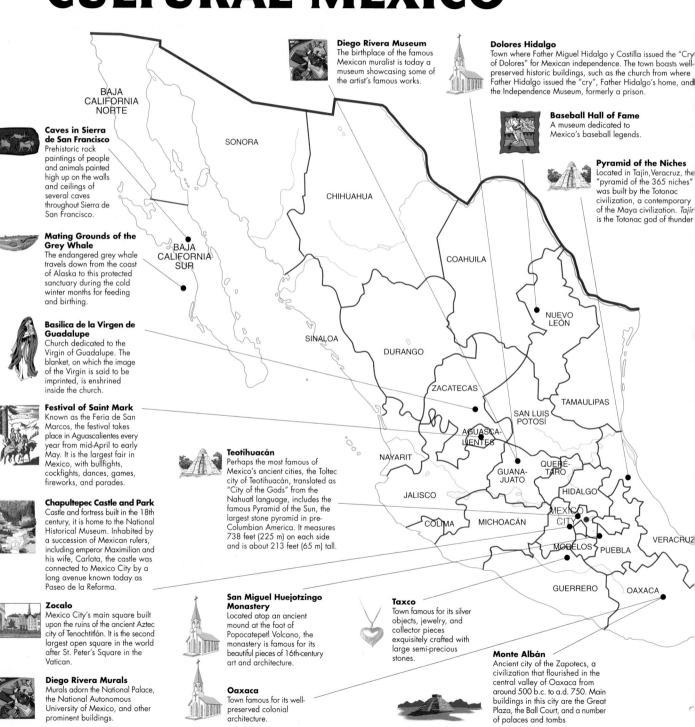

Diego Rivera Museum
The birthplace of the famous Mexican muralist is today a museum showcasing some of the artist's famous works.

Dolores Hidalgo
Town where Father Miguel Hidalgo y Costilla issued the "Cry of Dolores" for Mexican independence. The town boasts well-preserved historic buildings, such as the church from where Father Hidalgo issued the "cry", Father Hidalgo's home, and the Independence Museum, formerly a prison.

Baseball Hall of Fame
A museum dedicated to Mexico's baseball legends.

Pyramid of the Niches
Located in Tajín, Veracruz, the "pyramid of the 365 niches" was built by the Totonac civilization, a contemporary of the Maya civilization. *Tajín* is the Totonac god of thunder

BAJA CALIFORNIA NORTE

SONORA

CHIHUAHUA

Caves in Sierra de San Francisco
Prehistoric rock paintings of people and animals painted high up on the walls and ceilings of several caves throughout Sierra de San Francisco.

Mating Grounds of the Grey Whale
The endangered grey whale travels down from the coast of Alaska to this protected sanctuary during the cold winter months for feeding and birthing.

BAJA CALIFORNIA SUR

COAHUILA

NUEVO LEÓN

Basilica de la Virgen de Guadalupe
Church dedicated to the Virgin of Guadalupe. The blanket, on which the image of the Virgin is said to be imprinted, is enshrined inside the church.

SINALOA

DURANGO

ZACATECAS

SAN LUIS POTOSÍ

TAMAULIPAS

Festival of Saint Mark
Known as the Feria de San Marcos, the festival takes place in Aguascalientes every year from mid-April to early May. It is the largest fair in Mexico, with bullfights, cockfights, dances, games, fireworks, and parades.

AGUASCA-LIENTES

Teotihuacán
Perhaps the most famous of Mexico's ancient cities, the Toltec city of Teotihuacán, translated as "City of the Gods" from the Nahuatl language, includes the famous Pyramid of the Sun, the largest stone pyramid in pre-Columbian America. It measures 738 feet (225 m) on each side and is about 213 feet (65 m) tall.

NAYARIT

GUANA-JUATO

QUERÉ-TARO

HIDALGO

Chapultepec Castle and Park
Castle and fortress built in the 18th century, it is home to the National Historical Museum. Inhabited by a succession of Mexican rulers, including emperor Maximilian and his wife, Carlota, the castle was connected to Mexico City by a long avenue known today as Paseo de la Reforma.

JALISCO

COLIMA

MICHOACÁN

MEXICO CITY

MORELOS

PUEBLA

VERACRUZ

Zocalo
Mexico City's main square built upon the ruins of the ancient Aztec city of Tenochtitlán. It is the second largest open square in the world after St. Peter's Square in the Vatican.

GUERRERO

OAXACA

San Miguel Huejotzingo Monastery
Located atop an ancient mound at the foot of Popocatepetl Volcano, the monastery is famous for its beautiful pieces of 16th-century art and architecture.

Taxco
Town famous for its silver objects, jewelry, and collector pieces exquisitely crafted with large semi-precious stones.

Monte Albán
Ancient city of the Zapotecs, a civilization that flourished in the central valley of Oaxaca from around 500 b.c. to a.d. 750. Main buildings in this city are the Great Plaza, the Ball Court, and a number of palaces and tombs

Diego Rivera Murals
Murals adorn the National Palace, the National Autonomous University of Mexico, and other prominent buildings.

Oaxaca
Town famous for its well-preserved colonial architecture.

ABOUT THE CULTURE

Chichén Itzá
One of the most spectacular of Mexico's ancient cities, Chichén Itzá was built by the Maya civilization. It includes the famous Castillo pyramid, the Caracol temple, the Ball Court, as well as many rock carvings of snakes and jaguars.

Uxmal
Located in the midst of the tropical jungle, the ancient city of Uxmal was built by the Maya civilization. Its impressive structures include the Temple of the Magician pyramid, the House of the Turtles, the Ball Court, and the Nunnery.

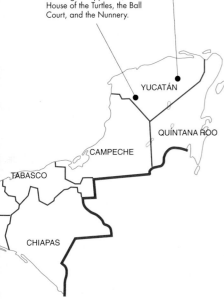

OFFICIAL NAME
Estados Unidos Mexicanos, United Mexican States

CAPITAL
Mexico City

DESCRIPTION OF FLAG
Three vertical bars of green, white, and red with a crest on the white panel of an eagle sitting on top of a cactus devouring a snake.

POPULATION
101.9 million (July 2001)

ETHNIC GROUPS
Amerindian 30%, Caucasian 9%, Mestizo (Amerindian-Spanish) 60%, others 1%

LIFE EXPECTANCY
Male 68, female 75 (1999)

INFANT MORTALITY RATE
Thirty-one per 1,000 live births (1999)

NATIONAL ANTHEM
Mexicanos, al Grito de Guerra ("Mexicans, at the Cry of War")

LITERACY RATE
Male and female 90 percent

EDUCATION
Government expenditure on education: 4.6% of GDP
Daily newspaper circulation per 1,000 people: 97

LEADERS IN THE ARTS
Carlos Fuentes, Octavio Paz (literature), Frida Kahlo, Diego Rivera (fine arts)

NATIONAL HOLIDAYS
New Year's Day—Jan. 1
Constitution Day—Feb. 5
Birthday of Benito Juarez— Mar. 21
Good Friday—Mar./Apr.*
Easter Monday—Mar./Apr.*
Labor Day—May 1
Cinco de Mayo—May 5
Independence Day—September 15 and 16
Day of Race—Oct. 12
All Saints' Day—Nov. 1
Memorial Day—Nov. 2
Revolution Day—Nov. 20
Our Lady of Guadalupe Day— Dec. 12
Christmas Day—Dec. 25
*Exact date established according to lunar calendar.

POLITICS
System of government: constitutional republic
Current leader: Vicente Fox Quesada (elected in 2000)
Next elections: 2006

TIME LINE

IN MEXICO	IN THE WORLD

753 B.C.
Rome founded

300 B.C.
Monte Albán Civilization appears in southern Mexico

34 B.C.
Death of Plato, Ancient Greek philosopher

200 B.C.
Teotihuacán Civilization appears in central Mexico

116–17 B.C.
Roman Empire reaches its greatest extent, under Emperor Trajan (98-17)

200 A.D.
Mayan Civilization appears in Yucatan Peninsula

600 A.D.
Height of Mayan civilization

1376
First Aztec king crowned

1000
Chinese perfect gunpowder and begin to use it in warfare

1440–68
Reign of Aztec emperor Moctezuma I

1502–1520
Reign of Moctezuma II

1519–1521
Hernán Cortés and 500 of his men conquer the Aztec Empire

1530
Beginning of trans-Atlantic slave trade organized by Portuguese in Africa

1521–1550
Spanish colonial administration established

1550–1600
Ranching, industry, and mining expand

1558–1603
Reign of Elizabeth I of England

1600–1700
Economic stagnation in colony and racial stratification established

1620
Pilgrim Fathers sail the Mayflower to America

1681
Frenchman LaSalle explores Mississippi river from source to mouth, and founds Louisiana

1700–1800
Bourbon monarchs in Spain revitalize the colony

1776
U.S. Declaration of Independence

1789–1799
The French Revolution

1810
Miguel Hidalgo makes cry for independence

1821
Mexican independence declared

1836
Texas becomes independent from Mexico

IN MEXICO	IN THE WORLD
1846 • Mexican–American War begins	
1853 • President Santa Ana sells additional territory to the United States—the Gadsden Purchase	
1858–1861 • Conflict over President Benito Juarez's reforms	• **1861** U. S. Civil War begins
1862–1866 • French intervention in Mexico	• **1869** The Suez Canal is opened
1910 • Rebellion against Porfirio Díaz's rule	• **1914** World War I begins
1927 • Constitution of 1917 amended to extend presidential term to six years	• **1939** World War II begins
1940 • Mexico declares war on the Axis powers	• **1945** The United States drops atomic bombs on Hiroshima and Nagasaki
	• **1949** North Atlantic Treaty Organization (NATO) formed
1952–1958 • Women's suffrage extended to the national level	• **1957** Russians launch Sputnik
	• **1966–1969** Chinese Cultural Revolution
1970–1976 • Oil boom in Chiapas and Tabasco	• **1986** Nuclear power disaster at Chernobyl in Ukraine
	• **1991** Break-up of Soviet Union
1992 • North American Free Trade Agreement (NAFTA) is signed between Mexico, Canada, and the United States	
1994 • NAFTA takes effect; the Zapatista Guerrilla movement begins in Chiapas	• **1997** Hong Kong is returned to China
2000 • Vicente Fox Quesada is elected president	• **2001** World population surpasses 6 billion

GLOSSARY

atole ("ah-TOH-lay")
A popular drink made from corn.

adobe
Sun-dried brick.

charrería ("char-RER-EE-ah")
Mexican-style rodeo.

charros ("CHAR-ros")
Mexican cowboys.

conquistadores ("kon-KEES-tah-dor-ehs")
The Spanish conquerors who colonized Mexico.

Creoles
People of Spanish descent born in Mexico.

ejidos ("eh-HEE-dohs")
Communal farmlands.

encomienda (*"ehn-koh-mee-ehn-dah"*)
Spanish colonial system which granted Spanish settlers a large area of land in the American colonies in exchange for paying taxes to the Spanish king and converting the Amerindian population to Christianity.

haciendas (*"ah-see-EHN-dahs"*)
Large plantations.

machismo ("mah-CHEES-moh")
Aggressive behavior by men that emphasizes masculinity.

mestizo ("mehs-TEE-soh")
Person of mixed European and Indian ancestry.

peninsulares ("pay-nin-SOO-lah-rehs")
Spaniards born in Spain but living in Mexico or other Spanish colonies in the Americas, usually representing the Spanish crown.

serape ("say-RAH-pay")
A colorful blanket.

siesta ("see-EHS-tah")
A short nap taken after the main meal of the day, usually for one or two hours.

zócalo ("SOH-kah-loh")
A central plaza or square around which villages and cities are organized. The *zócalo* is the center of the town's activities. The main plaza in Mexico City is simply called the Zócalo.

FURTHER INFORMATION

Books

Cruz, Barbara C. *Jose Clemente Orozco: Mexican Artist.* Berkeley Heights: Enslow
    Publishers, Inc., 1998.

Gerson, Mary-Joan. *Fiesta Femenina: Celebrating Women in Mexican Folktales.* Cambridge:
    Barefoot Books, 2001.

McGee, Charmayne. *So Sings the Blue Deer.* New York: Atheneum-MacMillan Pub., 1997.

Rochfort, Desmond. *Mexican Muralists: Orozco, Rivera, Siqueiros.* San Francisco: Chronicle
    Books, 1998.

Rosales, Francisco A. *Chicano!: The History of the Mexican American Civil Rights
    Movement.* Houston: Arte Público Press, University of Houston, 1997.

Shalant, Phyllis. *Look What We've Brought You From Mexico: Crafts, Games, Recipes,
    Stories, and Other Cultural Activities from Mexican-Americans.* New York: Julian
    Messner, 1992.

Zannos, Susan. *Cesar Chavez: A Real-Life Reader Biography.* Bear: Mitchell Lane
    Publishers, Inc., 1998.

Videos

Americas. Boston: Boston and Central Television, 1993.

Imagining New Worlds. London: BBC for the Open University, 1995.

Mexico: A Story of Courage and Conquest. New York: The History Channel, 1999.

Websites

@migo! Mexico; general information plus kid's page. Http://www.mexonline.com/

Mexico's facts and figures. Http://www.ilap.com/~tgmag/ap/apmex.html

Mexico for tourists and those interested in history. Http://mexico.udg.mx/ingles.html

Kid's page hosted by the government of Mexico; includes information and games in
    English and Spanish. Http://www.elbalero.gob.mx

News about environmental and human rights issues in Mexico. Http://www.
    globalexchange.org/campaigns/mexico/

BIBLIOGRAPHY

Cramer, Mark. *Culture Shock! Mexico*. Portland: Graphic Arts Center Publishing Company, 2001.

Hall, Barbara J. *Mexico in Pictures*. New York: Sterling Publishing Company, 1987.

Muller, Kal and Garcia-Oropeza, Guillermo. *Insight Guides: Mexico*. New York: Prentice Hall Travel, 1989.

Oster, Patrick. *The Mexicans: A Personal Protrait of a People*. New York: William Morrow and Company, 1989.

Http://www.odci.gov/cia/publications/factbook/geos/mx.html

Http://www.state.gov/www/background_notes/mexico_0101_bgn.html

INDEX